small is beautiful
in the 21st century

Photo © Sophie Baker

Schumacher Briefing No. 17

small is beautiful in the 21st century

the legacy of E. F. Schumacher

Diana Schumacher

Published by Green Books
for The Schumacher Society

First published in 2011
by Green Books Ltd
Dartington Space, Dartington Hall, Totnes, Devon TQ9 6EN
www.greenbooks.co.uk

for The Schumacher Society
The CREATE Centre, Smeaton Road, Bristol BS1 6XN
www.schumacher.org.uk   admin@schumacher.org.uk

Printed by TJ International Ltd, Padstow, Cornwall, UK

Text printed on 100% recycled paper
Covers printed on 75% recycled material

A catalogue record for this publication is available from the British Library.

ISBN 978 1 900322 75 1

The Schumacher Briefings
Founding Editor: Herbert Girardet

Contents

Acknowledgements

This Schumacher Briefing could not have been published in its present form without the very significant input and contributions from the following people, who are listed alphabetically. I am indebted to each of them personally for their encouragement and inspiration, but more importantly for the part they are collectively playing in the emerging tapestry of humanity's future.

Godric Bader (the Scott Bader Commonwealth); John Elford (Green Books); John Fullerton (The New Economics Institute, USA); Dr G.K. Giri (Schumacher Centre for Development); Michael Gordon (The New Economics Institute, USA); Peter Harper (Centre for Alternative Technology); Patrick Holden (Formerly of the Soil Association); Satish Kumar (Resurgence Magazine / Schumacher College / The Small School); George McRobie (ex-Chairman of ITDG, India Development Group, Soil Association); Brian Padgett (formerly ITDG–AT); Andrew Redpath (Jeevika Trust); Ian Roderick (Schumacher Institute); Sir Julian Rose (International Coalition to Protect the Polish Countryside); Richard St George (Schumacher Society); Peter Segger (Soil Association); Lily Swan (New Economics Foundation (**nef**)); Simon Trace (Practical Action); Stewart Wallis (New Economics Foundation); Susan Witt (The New Economics Institute, USA); and Laszlo Zsolnai (Corvinus University of Budapest). I am also grateful to all those, too numerous to mention here, who have given insight and inspiration.

My thanks to Stephen Powell for his comments on the first draft of this Briefing, and especially to John Elford, Green Books editor and publisher, for all his sound advice and, above all, for his infinite patience! My gratitude to all those who have kindly read each chapter and have given comment and advice, and to Pam Brabner for conscientiously typing successive drafts and updates. Last but not least, I would like to thank my husband Christian, the eldest son of Fritz Schumacher, who has read through and commented on each chapter, as well as giving much practical help, encouragement, and support.

My profound thanks to Verena Schumacher, Fritz's widow, for allowing me to use copyrighted material from his writings; and to Barbara Wood, his daughter, for use of the biographical information in *Alias Papa*, her biography of her father.

It has been difficult to keep up to date with all the developments of the organisations directly associated with the work of E. F. Schumacher, and to do them justice within this limited space. I apologise for any omissions, and take full responsibility for any oversights or errors.

It is my hope that the information on the ongoing work and relevance of Fritz Schumacher today will encourage and inspire readers to take up the challenge of transforming their world for the better in whatever way seems most appropriate to their circumstances, or through supporting one or other of the organisations mentioned in this Briefing. Please circulate this publication as widely as possible amongst your friends and through your own networks. Thank you also for your own support and action!

Diana Schumacher
Godstone, 2011

Chapter 1

Who was E. F. Schumacher?

"Knowledge that does not help people to overcome their problems and to lead to a better and happier life is no use." – Dr A.T. Ariyaratne

Ernst Friederich (Fritz) Schumacher, the economist-philosopher, was an unlikely pioneer of the Green Movement. He was born in Bonn in 1911, studied at Oxford as a Rhodes Scholar and returned to England before the Second World War to avoid living under Nazism. He died prematurely on a lecture visit to Caux, Switzerland, in September 1977.

Coming from a distinguished intellectual background (his father was the first Professor of Economics at Berlin University), Schumacher himself experienced a short but meteoric academic career in Germany, England and America, becoming assistant lecturer in banking and international finance at Columbia University at the age of 23. However, he always believed that one should strive for practical outcomes to philosophy and economic theory which would benefit people and society. In both his outer and his inner life he was a searcher for truth and dedicated to peace and non-violence. Unlike so many of his contemporary academics, however, he wanted to see these ideals translated into practical actions and right livelihoods.

He saw the need to provide his colleagues and audiences with philosophical 'maps' and guidelines which related to reality. In the process, his life was one of constant questioning, including challenging most of the basic assumptions on which Western economic and academic theory have been based. What are the 'laws' that govern the 'science' of economics? What is the true value of money? What is the relationship between time and money? What is the real worth of work? And of development? These were the everyday questions which interested him most as an economist. Gradually he saw the need to expand the vision of contemporary economists to put human wellbeing at the centre of economic decision-making and everything within the context of environmental sustainability.

Part of Fritz Schumacher's personal sorrow – but analytical strength and objectivity – lay in the fact that he remained 'an outsider' for most of his life. He never fully integrated with his fellow students either in England or Germany, or with any particular community or sect. His original thinking and academic successes only set him further apart from his contemporaries, despite his humorous good nature and obvious talents. Early commercial assignments ranged from Wall Street to the City of London, to organising an independent and lucrative barter import-export enterprise run from Germany during the pre-war depression.

In 1937, owing to Hitler's frenzied ascendancy and his own feeling of the intellectual and political betrayal of Germany and its heritage by his nationalistic compatriots, he decided to abandon the majority of his social, family and business ties and to bring his young wife and son to London, where he was granted British citizenship. He was certain that until Germany could be purged of the Nazis' evil presence there would be no peace in Europe; but that ultimately the reconstruction of Europe might be led from England. He hoped that he would then be in a position to be the vanguard of social and economic reform in Germany. Because of anti-German feeling among the English at the time, his work was not recognised publicly.

A second son arrived during the war, and the young Schumacher family faced the hostility of being regarded as German aliens. They had to give up their home, and after being briefly interned, Fritz was hidden away with his family in Northamptonshire, working as a farm labourer, and was referred to by the very English name of James. At the same time and with the support of J. M. Keynes, Schumacher was seconded to do government research at the Oxford Institute of Statistics whilst at the same time working on his own 'world improvement schemes'.[1] Throughout the war years he worked on ideas of debt relief, international debt clearing schemes and solutions to international trade deficits. Sometimes his ideas were appropriated by others, such as his contribution to the Beveridge Report in the early 1940s and to the Marshall Plan of 1947. Although he never received official recognition for his input to such prestigious schemes, this did not disquiet him. The most important aspect of all intellectual and research experience, in his view, was to get the necessary ideas implemented by whoever was best able to effect them.

During and immediately after the Second World War, Schumacher was also frequently invited to write for *The Observer, The Times, The Economist* and other mainstream publications, at first under pseudonyms, since the editors feared that the German name would offend. It was many years later that he was able to put his own name to his writing. Immediately after the war he was appointed Economic Adviser to the Allied Control Commission, and was sent back to Germany where many of his relatives and friends regarded the now naturalised English family as having 'deserted the sinking ship'. As he once sadly remarked, "I am a fellow without a fatherland."

Although the expanding family was again domiciled in England from 1950 onwards (Fritz was now Economic Adviser to the newly nationalised National Coal Board), his quest for patterns of sustainability took him all over the world. He had experienced poverty, social injustice and alienation first-hand, and felt that with his uniquely varied and practical background he had something useful to contribute. As an economist he was derided by his peers for pointing out the fallacy of continuous growth in a finite world dependent on limited fossil fuel resources, but at the same time he became a champion of the poor, the marginalised and those who felt misgivings over the shallowness of contemporary values. This made him a cult figure of the hippie movement in the late 1960s and early 1970s, with over 5,000 students attending some of the lectures he gave in California on his last visit to the United States in 1977.

Philosophy and religion

From his youth Fritz had always read prolifically. He was influenced by many different philosophers and thinkers and his personal library contained an eclectic selection of books – from Socrates to Shakespeare; from Marx to Chairman Mao; from R. H. Tawney to Einstein; from Adam Smith to J. M. Keynes. He also read widely the great sages of all the world's religions. Yet one of the people who influenced him most was Leopold Kohr,[2] whose views on the appropriate size of nation states and political structures greatly informed his own philosophy of appropriate-scale institutions and technology.

At one stage or another during his life, Fritz questioned all the main traditions, whether intellectual, national, economic or religious. As a young man he claimed to be a dedicated atheist, lecturing that religion and morality were mere products of history; they did not stand up to scientific examination and could be modified if regarded as inappropriate. Politically he was a loving socialist, the antithesis to Hitler's fascism, and an idealist with a restless mind. His economic values were very modern, based on the speed, measurement, efficiency and logic of the industrialised Western world which he inhabited. It was only later that he understood that such criteria were too inflexible, and totally incompatible with the more subtle 'unconscious' rhythms of the natural world. As a commuter from suburban Caterham (where he eventually lived) to the National Coal Board headquarters in London's Victoria (where he worked from 1950 to 1970), he used the train travelling time to study comparative religions and, among other great thinkers, was greatly influenced by the German philosopher Fritjof Schuon's *The Transcendent Unity of Religions*.[3]

This period of commuting to work proved a most fruitful turning point in Schumacher's inner life. He first studied notably those religions from the East, attending meetings and lectures on the spirituality of other faiths, and began to practise meditation.[4] Gradually he came to relinquish the atheism of his youth, and to admit to the possibility of a 'Higher Order of Being'. His changing economic and metaphysical views (which sometimes seemed contradictory) chronologically mirrored his own spiritual struggles and development. There was, after all, a transcendent 'vertical perspective' to life – a hierarchy of orders from inanimate matter through different levels of consciousness to a supreme consciousness or Being.

In 1960 Schumacher's first wife died and he married Verena Rosenberg. The four children of each marriage were brought up in the Christian faith. After years of searching and inner struggles he had realised a way of bringing his lifelong paths of study and social concerns to a point of convergence, and had reached his own spiritual homecoming. Finally, to the astonishment of Schumacher's Marxist, Buddhist and Christian friends alike, he was received into the Roman Catholic Church in 1971, six years before he died. It was a formal renouncement of his previously cherished views of the supremacy of the intellect and reason over the Christian virtues of compassion, forgiveness, unconditional love, the acknowledgement of a Divine Creator, and the integrity of all creation.

Burma and 'Buddhist Economics'

In 1955, whilst working at the National Coal Board, Schumacher accepted a three-month assignment as Economic Development Adviser to the Government of the Union of Burma, where he immediately attached himself to a Buddhist monastery. He soon concluded that the last thing the Burmese people needed was economic development along Western lines. They needed an economics suited to their own culture and lifestyle – a 'middle way' between the Western model which sought to increase material wants and consumption, to be satisfied through mechanised production, and the Buddhist model which was to satisfy basic human needs through dignified work, which also purified one's character and was a spiritual offering. The tools of economic development therefore had to be adapted to people's needs and values, and not vice versa. Unsurprisingly, his report was not well received in official quarters and he was never invited back.

However, the Burmese experience proved a seminal turning point in Fritz's spiritual and intellectual development: it also brought together many of the separate strands in his life, particularly those relating to economic development in the Third World. He was later to coin the term 'Buddhist Economics'[5] which, like Marxism, implies a complete rejection of the greed and materialism on which so much of modern economics is based, and also a respect for the value and dignity of meaningful work. This 'middle way' became the basis of Schumacher's approach to technology as well as development planning. His Buddhist experience also opened the door to his later studies of Eastern mysticism and Western religions, and eventually through St Augustine, Thomas Aquinas and the early Church Fathers, to Christianity.

Sustainable development

In tandem with his job at the Coal Board, Schumacher also undertook an intensive programme of international travel, initially to give substance to his proposals to save the collapsing British coal industry. His aim was to encourage independence from the Western world's industrial reliance on cheap imported coal and oil imports from the Middle East. Alas – and to our cost today – he was successful in neither, and most UK coalmines were closed. Subsequent to his death, the North Sea oil and gas industries were developed and sold off, rendering the nation today dependent on imported fuels.

His aim was also to promote sustainable development strategies in the First and Third World alike, travelling extensively in the USA, Canada, Latin America, Africa and India, as well as to Japan and Russia (although he never lived to see the end of the Cold War). Fuel and food he saw as the two basic necessities for survival and sustainability. All communities and regions should strive to be self-sufficient in these as far as possible – otherwise they become economically and politically vulnerable. In this respect he was an early proponent of harnessing renewable energy in all its different forms, upgrading the existing traditional energy-generating technologies and exploring potential new developments and technologies.

Unfortunately Fritz was many years ahead of his time, and few policy-makers took much notice. Putting his own self-sufficiency theories into practice, his was one of the first UK houses to have solar panels installed on its roof. He also personally became involved in sustainable agriculture, an enthusiasm which he claimed had its seeds in his work as a farm labourer. He spent much time on his organic garden, was President of the UK Soil Association, and was an unflagging advocate of tree-planting and forest farming schemes wherever he went. He lost no opportunity to warn against soil impoverishment, the erosion and ecological degradation that follows forest-felling schemes, or of economic dependence of agricultural systems based on monocultures and oil-based chemical fertilisers. The last month of his life saw him making a film in Western Australia in the hope of defending the native forests from overseas logging interests.[6] He viewed the clear-felling of forests – whether for timber, pulp or monoculture crops – as the very antithesis of sustainable development.

Intermediate technology

It was during an official visit to India in 1961 to advise the Indian Government on a Five-Year Development Plan, that Fritz became deeply moved by the hopeless poverty and deprivation of countless thousands of people. He realised that nearly all the official government and other Western aid schemes proposed so far were completely inadequate, as the money did not filter down to poor communities. What poor people needed was 'tool aid' and 'know-how' – simple improvements to their traditional tools and technical support to use their local assets more effectively. This concept became known as 'intermediate' or 'appropriate' technology, and is described in Chapter 3.

Industry and business in developed countries

In 1950 Schumacher joined the National Coal Board as their Economic Adviser. He had accepted the position partly because of his strong socialist convictions, his sympathy with the miners and his belief that true economic sustainability for industrial countries would most readily come about through the proper organisation and use of energy resources. He was also an early advocate of the principle of subsidiarity, and realised that the workers themselves needed to operate within 'human-scale' structures even in large organisations. The National Coal Board, he hoped, would be an excellent springboard for testing his ideas in practice. Schumacher was also particularly struck by the model of the Scott Bader Commonwealth, a plastics and polymers company located in Northamptonshire, whose Board he eventually joined in 1967. The innovative structures of ownership in this organisation are described in Chapter 7.

Publications

Despite growing recognition of Schumacher's ideas through numerous projects, broadcasts, writings, pamphlets and public lectures, the real breakthrough only came with the publication in 1973 of his first book *Small is Beautiful: A Study of Economics as if People Mattered.*[7] This was written in layman's terms, since it was mainly based on previous lectures and articles, but it somehow caught the spirit of the times. *Small is Beautiful* was not just about appropriate size. It articulated what millions of 'little people' worldwide subconsciously believed: that unlike any previous culture or civilisation, twentieth-century Western society, whether agricultural or industrial, was living artificially off the Earth's capital rather than off its income. Its lifeblood was the ever-increasing use of non-renewable resources – primarily by the rich countries at the expense of the poor. The world could not continue sustainably on the increasing curve of production and consumption without material or moral restraint. His colleague George McRobie later followed this message up with the highly practical book of examples mainly taken from the Intermediate Technology Development Group (ITDG) in *Small is Possible.*[8]

Schumacher's simple yet provocative style of communication inspired many people to question the future and the values of the market-led consumerist society, and to make radical changes in their own lifestyles. It was, however, his personal commitment and dedication which kindled enthusiasm and gave those whom he met the courage to change. This message of empowerment had unusual resonance worldwide: from President Carter of the USA, who summoned him to the White House in 1977, to Prince Charles and the Duke of Edinburgh and to countless thousands of dispossessed people in the Third World. He exhorted all to rely on 'people power' and their own mental and physical inventiveness, rather than basing their futures on imported capital and energy-intensive technologies which reduce need for the human workforce. The message still flies in the face of most prevailing political and economic policies today, but has had a profound influence on very many organisations and institutions including those represented in this Briefing.

Fritz Schumacher's second book, *A Guide for the Perplexed*,[9] followed in 1977. In it he outlined his deepest spiritual beliefs, and it was the distillation of his lifelong search for truth. Other publications such as *Good Work*,[10] *Schumacher on Energy*[11] and *This I Believe*[12] were produced posthumously and were based on his earlier writings in different publications and journals, including *Resurgence* magazine.

The strength of Schumacher's arguments still lies in the timeless spiritual wisdom they represent, and in his exceptional ability to address problems at the systems level and to communicate solutions simply and practically. His message was an inclusive one: "Do not break down problems into isolated components, but look at the world and see it whole". It is only a complete metanoia in all departments of life, rather than engaging in an 'over-extending battle with symptoms', which will educate us to change sufficiently fundamentally so that we can avoid the universal breakdown which we face in today's society.

Chapter 2

The Schumacher Society: its origins and offshoots

"The slenderest knowledge that may be obtained of the highest things is more desirable than the most certain knowledge of lesser things."
— St. Thomas Aquinas

For Schumacher, education was the most vital of all human resources since he considered the human mind the key factor in all development. For him, however, the world of education as he had experienced it was essentially lacking: it accorded no place to metaphysics, made no distinction between convergent and divergent problems, and took no account of the higher truths which are needed to guide and direct our lives through complex situations. His view was that:

"All subjects [studied], no matter how specialised, are connected with a centre; . . . they are like rays emanating from a sun . . . . the centre consists of metaphysics and ethics, of ideas that – whether we like it or not – transcend the world of facts." [1]

Education, he argued, can only help if it produces 'whole' people who are truly in touch with this centre, and have therefore acquired not only knowledge but wisdom and a proper sense of values. These, in turn, will help them transcend the divergent problems of life – the reconciliation of opposites – with the higher power of love.

Schumacher believed that people's minds and the harnessing of their inherent ingenuity are one of the greatest resources of any society, and therefore a system of education which developed the whole person was all-important. In these ideas he was also greatly influenced by the ideas of Gandhi, educating children also in practical skills and spiritual values so as to become responsible contributors to the society in which they live. He was also an admirer of Ivan Illich, the controversial former Jesuit priest from whose book *Deschooling Society*[2] he often quoted. He believed that the core purpose of education is the transmission of ideas of value: "ideas which people think and feel, much transcend mere facts and statistics." Education therefore, must be people-centred, always with a spiritual and higher dimension in view.

He frequently compared his own school and university education to a map he had been given on a visit to Leningrad during the Cold War. When he enquired why there were no churches marked, his guide explained that the policy was to show none of the 'living churches' but only those which now served some other purpose, such as housing museums or schools. He later observed:

> *"All through school and university I had been given maps of life and knowledge on which there was hardly a trace of any of the things that I most cared about and that seemed to me to be of the greatest possible importance to the conduct of my life."*[3]

The Schumacher Society

After Fritz Schumacher died in 1977, it was Satish Kumar who galvanised Christian (Fritz's eldest son) and myself, together with some of Fritz's closest intellectual supporters in the UK, to form a 'Schumacher Society'. The initial purpose would be publicising and developing Schumacher's ideas; and encouraging networking with like-minded individuals and groups involved in the emerging environmental movement.

It was decided that the Society would be formed as a not-for-profit company focused on education and managed by a Council. The original Council was, indeed, a vibrant group of leading environmental thinkers and activists, all of whom had known Schumacher personally. Maurice Ash (then chairman of the Dartington Hall Trust and a dedicated social entrepreneur) was the Society's initial chairman. The first meeting took place in a pub in West Wales, where the group agreed to offer their time, money and resources until the Society could afford to pay for a part-time administrator and rent an office. All Council members still give their time, travel and associated costs free. The costs of running the Bristol office and a part-time administrator were met through membership subscriptions, donations and from the sales of Schumacher Lecture tickets and publications.

Once it had been decided to establish a Schumacher Society, it seemed fitting that the primary focus of the Society should be to work towards a more holistic system of education in its various forms. These included experiments in many different dimensions through publications, lectures and through exploring alternative models of educational institution which could serve as examples.

Resurgence magazine

Resurgence is a bi-monthly magazine which has become an influential part of the environmental and eco-spiritual movement. Originally conceived and edited by John Papworth and launched in 1966, in its early days it aimed to promote the interlinked ideas of a decentralised social, economic and political order, and to educate and stimulate creative debate. Schumacher had supported the initiative from its beginning, contributing in total some 35 articles, a selection of which were later collected into a book under the title of *This I Believe* edited by John Elford.

In 1973 Papworth had a sudden assignment overseas, and asked Schumacher to look after the magazine while he was away, as they both wanted to ensure the future of this inspiring and thought-provoking venture. Schumacher in turn invited Satish Kumar, a young Indian peace activist working in London, to temporarily take over the editorship as he was finding himself too busy for this added responsibility.

Originally Satish's editorship of *Resurgence* was intended to last only two years, but he has remained the magazine's very creative editor ever since. Together with a dedicated team, Satish and his wife June built up the journal from its original idealistic and radical beginnings, to the glossy international publication it is today, whilst still retaining the original spirit and ethos. To quote Satish:

"I have tried to bring, in an implicit way, Gandhian values to the maga-zine. For me, these values are in the trinity of soil, soul and society. In every issue we present articles which address the issues of environment, spirituality and social justice. But without poetry and aesthetics there can be no ecology and spirituality, so we bring in the arts, poetry and short stories as well as straightforward essays and articles."

Resurgence also puts on public events and often shares features, articles and speakers with the Schumacher Society. It currently has a circulation of 15,000 as well as an increasing online membership. Comparatively recently it became a charitable trust to ensure its own long-term sustain-ability. In some ways *Resurgence* has become synonymous with the work of the Schumacher Society – partly because of the common historical roots, and also because it encapsulates the inseparable link between economy, ecology, equity and spirituality. For a list of articles and con-tributors please see the magazine's website: www.resurgence.org.

The Schumacher Lectures

Given that the agreed focus was to be education, in 1978 the newly constituted Society was forced to address one very salient question: with such slender resources amounting to people's generosity, time and goodwill, on which aspects of Schumacher's multi-faceted work should it focus – and which aspects were not covered by any other organisa-tion? It was decided to run an annual day of lectures in the spirit of Schumacher's philosophy, given by key thinkers and activists drawn from across the globe. The only common factor required was that they had a holistic and inspiring vision – and the ability to share and com-municate this with others. Bristol was chosen as the venue for these Schumacher Lectures in preference to London, in an attempt to create a centre of gravity for such ideas outside the capital.

The Bristol Schumacher Lectures continue to this day, drawing large audiences from all over Britain from many different backgrounds, interests and persuasions. They have become perhaps the country's most prominent forum for investigating cutting-edge alternative ideas, and have developed into an annual gathering of the UK environment movement. An informal organisation of voluntary helpers and stewards has grown up to guide the participants, look after speakers, oversee the stalls and sell tickets. The renowned lecturers often charge no fees, which helps to keep costs down, although travelling and accommodation expenses are paid by the Society.

As the lecturers have an international dimension, the Society is able to establish closer links with the work and thinking of like-minded organisations throughout the world. There is also a great emphasis on the practical implications of the ideas expressed, and effort is made to keep in touch with the speakers and their organisations or networks after their return and so to increase the Society's own outreach. Frequently invited lecturers also address other branches of the Schumacher Circle, participate in courses at Schumacher College, and have their lectures and subsequent articles published in *Resurgence*. The first few years of lectures were transcribed and edited by Satish Kumar, and published in two volumes in 1980[4] and 1984.[5] They included contributions from R. D. Laing, Amory Lovins, Ivan Illich, Fritjof Capra, Edward de Bono, Leopold Kohr, Hazel Henderson, Johan Galtung, Rupert Sheldrake, James Lovelock, Wendell Berry, Gary Snyder and the American Indian Chief, Russell Means. In keeping with the times, later contributions were recorded on video tapes and now on DVD, obtainable from the Schumacher Society office.

In 2008 the Society ran a joint event with Forum for the Future which took the form of a multi-faceted congress, with the theme 'Is Less More?' Bill McKibben, a prominent alternative economist from the United States, was the keynote speaker and used the occasion to launch his www.350.org website and campaign (the name comes from the research of NASA scientist James Hansen, who said in a 2007 paper that in order to stabilise global warming, CO_2 in the atmosphere must not be allowed to exceed 350 parts per million).

The new highly participative formula of the 2008 joint conference proved so successful that it was decided to adopt it in future. The 2009 event in Bristol was run in collaboration with the New Economics Foundation (**nef**) under the theme 'From the Ashes of the Crash: Rebuilding with the new economics' with Stewart Wallis, Director of **nef** in the Chair. The

2010 Conference was held jointly with another Circle member, the Centre for Alternative Technology in mid Wales. The 2011 Conference which will commemorate the Centenary of Schumacher's birth, promises to be a mega-event including contributions from all members of the Schumacher Circle as well as other prominent international speakers.

Regional events

In addition to the Bristol Schumacher Lectures, from time to time there have been regional lectures and also discussion groups and seminars in such centres as Leeds, Liverpool, Manchester, Cambridge, Hay-on-Wye, Oxford, Dublin and Leeds.

Schumacher Awards

In 1995, to belatedly celebrate the 21st anniversary of the publication of *Small is Beautiful*, an annual Schumacher Award was instigated for 'unsung heroes and heroines' of the Green movement. This Award continues to be given at the Annual Bristol Schumacher Lectures, and serves as a recognition of grassroots workers who are doing pioneering work in sustainability and often receiving little publicity or support. The 2008 award went to Rob Hopkins, founder of the Transition Movement, who has since gone on to receive much wider acclaim. Like Hopkins, many of these initiators of small projects and exemplary initiatives have since achieved national or even international status.

Schumacher Book Service

Another early project was the Schumacher Book Service, run from the *Resurgence* office in north Devon. This was to supply ecological and spiritual publications by post to those unable to obtain them easily. It was a particularly useful service before the days of the internet, especially for people living in remote rural or island locations. After the facility of ordering or downloading books on line became widespread, demand for the service fell and the remaining stock and contacts were handed over to Green Spirit Books.

Green Books

In 1985 Satish Kumar and others including myself had the idea of setting up a small publishing company, to fill a gap in the dissemination
of environmental literature. Some members of the Schumacher Society
Council, readers of *Resurgence* and several environmental organisations,
put up the very modest share capital required and Green Books was
born. The company was initially spearheaded and run by Satish from the
Resurgence office. The company published its first titles in early 1987, the
aim being to provide books across a range of environmental and spiritual
issues. The present publisher, John Elford, joined the company in early
1989, having previously worked in the publishing arm of Intermediate
Technology Development Group, and hence was an ideal director of the
new venture. Armed with his former experience, John has imaginatively
developed and built up the company along Schumacher's principles,
whilst keeping publications relevant to contemporary needs.

In the early years, the publications list centred around ecology and
the arts, green history and politics, and a few practical books such as
Robert Hart's *Forest Gardening* and *The Self-Build Book* by Jon Broome
and Brian Richardson. However, sales were limited since the importance of the environmental movement was still largely unrecognised by
the general public until relatively recently: consequently the finances
were somewhat dire for a considerable number of years!

Green Books has maintained its original vision and since those early
pioneering days, environmental issues have moved to centre stage. The
publications list now numbers over 260 titles, including some very
influential ones such as *The Growth Illusion: How Economic Growth Has
Enriched the Few, Impoverished the Many and Endangered the Planet* by
Richard Douthwaite; *Free to be Human: Intellectual Self-defence in the
Age of Illusions* by David Edwards; *Global Spin: the Corporate Assault
on Environmentalism* by Sharo Beder; *Wild Law: A Manifesto for Earth
Justice* by Cormac Cullinan and *The Transition Handbook: from oil
dependency to local resilience* by Rob Hopkins.[6] The latter has proved
to be a reference manual for an extraordinary new grassroots move-

ment which is enabling local communities to work out how to develop more local self-sufficiency in energy, oil, food and transport. In turn, the growing trend towards local self-reliance reduces carbon emissions and also enables localities to become much less dependent on the ever-declining amount of fossil fuels through the unnecessary transportation of people, goods and services. Green Books has also published four titles by Satish Kumar, including his acclaimed autobiography *No Destination,* and a series of practical manuals ranging from composting to cookery.

The company is also concerned with the environmental impact of the book production process itself, including the choice of printers and paper. For many years it only used paper with at least 75% recycled content, but recently for financial reasons it has started to use papers certified by the Forest Stewardship Council (FSC) rather than recycled paper for some books. The company only uses environmentally aware printers, who use vegetable-based rather than oil-based inks, and has a broad environmental commitment in terms of materials used and modes of travel used on business. Another of Green Books' publications is *Greening Your Office,* which has proved useful to other ethical companies. Located on the Dartington Estate, Green Books works closely with Schumacher College and with the Society in all its publications, John Elford also being one of the Schumacher Society's directors.

Schumacher Briefings

In 1998 it was decided that the Schumacher Society should produce a series of short factual publications to cover topics of public interest aimed primarily at policy and decision-makers, educationalists and those needing a short overview of a particular subject within the sustainability context. These have been commissioned and edited by Herbie Girardet, Stephen Powell and John Elford, and published by Green Books. For a full list of titles see www.schumacher.org.uk.

The Small School

In the last quarter of the twentieth century there was a move to practise so-called 'economies of scale' throughout the state education system. Many village schools were closed on the grounds that they were 'uneconomical', while other schools were amalgamated into larger units. Classroom sizes were increased so that fewer staff would be required, and larger and larger 'comprehensive schools' came into being. This often proved a false economy when it came to the quality of learning, the relationships within the classrooms, discipline and the general ethos of these 'education factories'.

The changes in educational policy and delivery made some members of the Schumacher Society actively reconsider the true nature of education: to develop the 'whole person', body, mind and spirit. Again, the educational ideas of Mahatma Gandhi proved fertile ground for a small-scale experiment which took root in the village of Hartland in north Devon. Here Satish Kumar, his wife June Mitchell and a group of parents and teachers decided to establish a small independent village secondary school to cater for pupils aged 11-16. This was backed and publicised by *Resurgence*, and in some ways was the Schumacher Society's earliest educational experiment. Once again, money was donated by members of the Society, readers of *Resurgence* and certain charitable trusts and organisations.

The focus of the Small School has always been to broaden the scope of learning into everyday life and the culture of the community. As well as mastering their academic subjects, passing the necessary state examinations and developing their intellectual skills, pupils also learn practical physical disciplines and techniques alongside the deeper underlying spiritual values. The integration of head, hands and heart in daily education originally made the 'Small School' approach unique in the UK.[7]

By 1982 £22,000 had been collected and Satish managed to purchase by auction a disused Methodist chapel in his village and to find a very enterprising headmaster from a comprehensive school who was willing to take the helm. Actively supported by parents, professionals and other members of the community, the Small School was established. Satish was Chairman of the Board of Governors and energetically engaged with parents in fundraising and publicity, both of which were necessary as the school was an independent non-selective community venture, with a bursary system for children from low income families.

In the first year there were only nine students from the locality, including the Kumars' own two children. In the following years the numbers reached 40, which was considered to be the maximum limit. In the school every child is valued as an individual and helped to develop according to his or her own particular interests and abilities in a caring co-operative environment. Although many who had heard about the Small School experiment wished to send their children from further afield (in one case, at least, from as far as Italy), it was decided that this would defeat the original purpose and that the school should serve only the immediate surrounding area. However, the school has hosted teachers and musicians from many parts of the world and, in turn, pupils have participated in a wide variety of overseas visits and projects. After attaining their GCSEs the majority of Small School pupils usually go on to some form of higher education.

Today attendance numbers fluctuate from between twenty-five and forty. The main ethos of the Small School is still to provide a holistic education for secondary school pupils in the locality. This saves the time and costs of a thirteen-mile bus journey each way to the nearest comprehensive school in Bideford. Often members of the local community with specialist knowledge or skills are prepared to teach the children, and develop particular interests that are not catered for by the three educationally qualified paid staff members. Extracurricular activities which have been covered in this way by members of the community include learning Arabic, many kinds of music, painting, pottery, gardening, building, drama, creative writing and photography.

At the school children prepare their own lunch every day (under supervision!), as the kitchen is not only a place to provide food but also a classroom for learning about nutrition and health. Understanding where food comes from, its dietary value and how to share the meal together with other pupils, teachers, parents and guests, is an integral part of the daily education. As the school has a garden, children also participate in the growing of food as well as in the cooking, dish-washing and cleaning. This was taking place long before the recent Jamie Oliver-inspired move for children nationwide to learn to grow and cook their school lunches.

Human Scale Education Movement

A number of other schools have sprung up on similar lines using the Small School as a model, and a Human Scale Education movement has since been launched to promote the idea of small schools around the country (www.hse.org.uk). Human Scale Education is a registered charity advising small and experimental schools as well as lobbying government to embrace the idea of reducing classroom sizes. Similar organisations have since started up in other countries, including the USA and The Netherlands.

Schumacher College

The College is another member of the Schumacher Circle – an innovative educational experiment in the widest sense, and closely associated with the Schumacher Society. In the early 1990s various interrelated systemic disciplines were emerging: these included Chaos theory, Complexity theory and Gaia theory on the one hand, and on the other a growing spiritual understanding of ecology and Deep Ecology as a response to an age of materialism and consumerism. There was a need for scholars and activists to critically explore and debate these new ideas in a relaxed and convivial environment.

Thus in 1991 Schumacher College was established on the Dartington Estate near Totnes in Devon, to provide space for those seeking personal transformation in their relationship with nature and to engage in mutual learning and discussion. The college, with the financial backing of the Dartington Hall Trust and various friends from the Society, was set up by Satish Kumar with some members of the Schumacher Council and close associates on the Advisory Board. As Fritjof Capra observed, "Until 1991 there was no centre of learning where ecology could be studied in a rigorous, in-depth way from so many different perspectives." [8]

Schumacher's essay on 'Buddhist Economics', frequently mentioned in this Briefing, was again one of the main inspirations behind the vision of the college. Indeed, Dr A. T. Ariyaratne, the renowned Gandhian peace worker from Sri Lanka and founder of the Sarvodaya peace movement, gave one of the earliest courses at the College on this topic. Dr Ariyaratne, who first met Fritz Schumacher in 1972, has been developing courses, lecturing and writing on Buddhist economics ever since. From 1993 until 2006 the College was run by Anne Phillips, the Administrative Director, together with Satish Kumar, who also teaches at the College. The short courses (from one to three weeks) are extremely wide-ranging – from economics to architecture, from permaculture to the arts, education and health – all from a holistic and interconnected perspective.

The College continues to attract students from all over the world (from over 80 countries to date), with each course bringing together a group of extremely dynamic and interesting participants from all walks of life. The resident teachers and lecturers are of the highest international calibre, the first 'scholar-in-residence' being James Lovelock, the renowned originator of Gaia Theory, followed by eminent thinkers and activists such as Jonathan Porritt, Vandana Shiva, Fritjof Capra, Wendell Berry, James Hillman, Manfred Max-Neef and others of similar stature (most of whom had given a Schumacher lecture in the past and hence are also Fellows of the Schumacher Society).

Schumacher College provides an opportunity for deep reflection and learning, but also is a catalyst for creativity – for doing and making. The participants and scholars-in-residence all interact as a single community for the duration of the course, engaging together in gardening, cooking, cleaning and other physical activities. There is always an enriching range of ages, experience and cultural backgrounds, and these now form part of an international network of colleagues, friends and activists. Learning from nature and the environment as well as from each other is also emphasised, and therefore residents experience weekly field trips on Dartmoor or to the sea in order to put this aspect of learning into practice. As Satish remarked, "One has to be in nature, and really get to know and love her first-hand, before any grounded ecological learning can take place."

The College operates on the Gaian premise that the Earth is a living organism and not a machine. Therefore a respect for the Earth is a first step towards studying the workings of the environment and society, and for many students the time they spent at the College has proved a pivotal turning point in their personal or career development. In addition, the college established the first recognised Masters degree programme in Holistic Science, which is accredited by the University of Plymouth. It now also offers a Certificate in Holistic Education, which is a year-long study programme.

Affiliated colleges

Inspired by the Schumacher College initiative, a number of affiliated projects have been developed in various countries, one of the most outstanding being Bija Vidyapeeth or 'Earth University' in India, (www. navdanya.org) founded in 1991 by Dr Vandana Shiva, the renowned physicist and activist, and Satish Kumar. It is a project of Navdanya, the 'School of the Seed', also founded by Vandana Shiva and situated on a 30-acre biodiversity farm in the foothills of the Himalayas near the city of Dehra Dun. It holds courses for farmers, women and young people as well as students coming from abroad.

While many of the learning activities at Bija Vidyapeeth are modelled on Schumacher College, here the emphasis is also on caring for the land, promoting organic agriculture and nutrition, water harvesting and community self-reliance. Vandana Shiva has been closely connected with the Schumacher Society and Schumacher College for very many years, and her own inspiring work provides yet another contemporary exemplar of Schumacher's 'learning to meet human needs from nature'.

Schumacher Institute for Sustainable Systems

In 2006 the Schumacher Society Council was approached by Ian Roderick with a proposal to set up a 'research institute' in Bristol which would be linked to the Society. The new research initiative would focus on sustainable systems, and draw together the experience and knowledge of people prominent in the field of systems theory. Members of the Council and friends of the Society were asked to subscribe seed funding for the project and thus the Schumacher Institute for Sustainable Systems was established, with Ian Roderick as its director.

It has held many seminars and workshops, and been involved with local sustainability initiatives, mainly in the south-west of the UK. Links with nearby universities have raised awareness of the Institute, and young people are offered internships, contributing their ideas and research work. The Institute now provides a place for learning, thought and personal development, and has funding for some paid research staff. One aspect of work with young people has since come to be known as 'Open Platform' (formerly 'Young Schumacher').

Go Zero

Go Zero, a project linked with the Schumacher Institute and The Converging World (see below), is based in the village of Chew Magna in Somerset and the surrounding area. This village initiative looks at how communities could move towards all aspects of zero waste. It is a collaborative inquiry, whereby all sections of the local community reflect on how to minimise waste at all levels, including energy and buildings – and people's own energy, talents and experience (this applies especially to young, unemployed and also retired people). The Institute provides technical support on energy efficiency and renewables. A derelict watermill in the village has been bought and restored, and is now also providing a community centre as well as office space for the project's headquarters. Other villages in the Chew Valley and elsewhere are following the same process. It is hoped that the experience of Go Zero might provide encouragement and an example for communities to reduce their environmental impact and carbon footprints (as with the zero carbon communities movement in the USA). The full story of Go Zero can be found in Schumacher Briefing no. 13, *Converging World*.[9]

The Converging World (TCW)

For much of its practical work and funding the Schumacher Institute is inextricably linked with The Converging World, an organisation set up in 2007 by John Pontin, Ian Roderick and others. A small subsection of the Go Zero Project formed The Converging World (TCW) Group. This was concerned not only with community waste but with our interconnectedness, and with the global picture of where waste was generated in other countries, frequently on our behalf. These wider aspects range from travel and transport to agriculture and production systems. TCW started off by committing to responsible travel and tourism as well as to fair trade. It then formed a partnership link to the Social Change and Development (SCAD) agency in southern India. With money raised mainly from donations and carbon-offset schemes, together they have funded wind turbines and other regeneration projects in some of the poorest villages of Tamil Nadu.

TCW is a very imaginative social enterprise, which uses the ideas of Contraction and Convergence to reduce the differences between rich and poor in their resource use, wealth and impact on the environment. The rich are encouraged to control their energy consumption and to reduce their carbon footprint. At the same time, by investing in local electrification schemes in poor regions overseas, people are enabled to improve their living and working conditions, hence increasing convergence across the globe. This, in turn, directly affects the twin issues of climate change and peak oil.

By investing in renewable energy generating systems and selling the electricity to the local authorities the two streams of revenue, from electricity and the sale of carbon credits, are used to pay for projects that will enable further convergence to take place. Representatives from both donor and recipient communities are encouraged to visit each other to share knowledge and know-how, and to feed these back to their own people – another aspect of convergence and a valuable linking process. In the words of John Pontin, "The issues we face are not a matter for governments to solve alone – the activities of millions of people working within their communities is essential." [10]

From its interdisciplinary thinking and implementation experience, the Institute has produced numerous reports and held seminars in many different locations. Details of these can be found on its website www.schumacherinstitute.org.

From this brief summary it will be appreciated that the Schumacher Society and its sister organisations have been the catalyst for a multitude of far-ranging initiatives, some of which have now developed into separate entities under the umbrella of the Schumacher Circle. A small but dedicated group of people, frequently volunteers, has been involved in building up an increasing number of activities over the years. The focus is not only on interpreting Fritz Schumacher's original ideas, but attempting to encourage, inspire and adapt them to contemporary needs and conditions.

The Schumacher Circle

In 1986 members of the Council expressed the desire to form closer ties with those other UK organisations which were in some way associated with the ideas and work of Schumacher. These were to become members of the Schumacher Circle, as already mentioned in the Introduction. The purpose of the Circle is to meet from time to time, and to share information, as well as participating in and promoting each other's events, publications and ideas. The E. F. Schumacher Society in America, our sister organisation, is a much valued affiliate member with whom we share information and frequently guest speakers and publications. In 2010 this Society, in association with **nef** (the New Economics Foundation in the UK), formed the New Economics Institute, which is based in Massachusetts and New York, (see pages 88-96). The work of other members of the Circle, whose history has not been directly connected with Schumacher UK, is outlined in the following chapters.

Chapter 3

Third World development models

Practical Action (formerly The Intermediate Technology Development Group) & Jeevika Trust (formerly India Development Group)

"Any intelligent fool can make things bigger, more complicated and more violent. It takes a touch of genius – and a lot of courage – to move in the opposite direction." – E. F. Schumacher

Background

On Fritz Schumacher's first visit to India in 1961 to speak on 'Paths to Economic Growth', he was confronted by his worst-ever experience of grinding and devastating poverty. In both rural areas and urban slums there was complete despair, malnutrition, degradation, apathy – a collapse of the local culture and of the human spirit. For some considerable time afterwards his mind was occupied as to why these poverty-stricken communities, who were not suffering the effects of war or sudden natural disaster, had lost all self-belief and seemed unable to help themselves or even utilise their own local resources. Even those areas which were recipients of national or international aid did not bear evidence of establishing any form of long-term sustainability.

The structural question that concerned Schumacher, in both the industrial and rural areas, was how to revive community life and production systems and to create new jobs in the cities whilst at the same time increasing villagers' sense of self-worth and independence. If this could only be solved, it would prevent the urban drift which both impoverishes village life and adds to the number of jobless slum dwellers, which in turn stresses and depletes the resources and the life of the cities. Schumacher observed that Western mass production technologies do not create jobs for the masses of poor people, but undercut in price even the modest goods produced by local artisans. Moreover, the two commodities which all these destitute communities have in abundance are time and labour – the very assets which modern technology is rapidly replacing. This situation still holds true today in many of the world's poorest communities, and many development agencies still continue to focus on introducing modern technology that is inappropriate to local needs.

After much persistent probing, Schumacher gradually concluded that attempts by the richer countries (and even by India's own central government) to give monetary aid or modern technology were simply misguided, as they were not reaching the rural poor or even the marginalised urban slum dwellers. A very small 'westernised' sector, now using modern methods of mass production, was operating in the cities, but was unintentionally creating a dual economy alongside the much greater numbers of traditional craftsmen and deprived agricultural workers. What was most needed to eradicate poverty was to revive and upgrade village industrial and agricultural methods whilst maintaining and valuing their traditional cultures.

Sophisticated Western technology was inaccessible to most of the Third World's poor, and did not create more rural workplaces. On the other hand, traditional tools and methods were frequently unreliable or inefficient and needed to be improved, as were the means of getting goods to market in the regions where there was absolutely no transport infrastructure. Also, there needed to be a corresponding transfer of knowledge and skills training to accompany the improved technologies. This would gradually increase productivity in the villages and stem the drift of unskilled jobless people into the cities.

Combining his Buddhist studies of 'the middle way' with Gandhian practicalities, Schumacher concluded that what was needed was an 'intermediate technology'. The poor needed technologies midway between their now uneconomical traditional methods and the costly high technology devices in which their governments were investing, or which were donated as aid and which only provided work for a very few. In order to make this middle way transition, again one had to 'find out what people do and help them do it better!'

To apply the concept of 'intermediate technology' required time to research into particular problems, to locate or invent the skills and tools appropriate to specific local needs, and to set up the necessary training and delivery systems. As a first practical step, George McRobie, Fritz's friend and colleague at the UK National Coal Board, who had an assignment in India with the Ford Foundation, agreed to assess the possibilities and practicalities and to build up a network of contacts. In 1965 the Intermediate Technology Development Group (ITDG) first met in London. The group started fundraising and, as a result of research, published its first buyer's guide for small-scale equipment entitled *Tools for Progress*. Gradually an international network of supporters was established – people and organisations who were committed to the power of Schumacher's ideas and their practical implementation. ITDG was officially registered as a charity in 1966, with Fritz as its founder/chairman. Its mission was to promote the role of 'technology with a human face' and 'people-centred development', and also to develop simple, more efficient tools and training for poor people in developing countries.

At the centre of Schumacher's thinking were care and respect for the millions of 'little people': people without status, without economic means and without a voice in their own destiny. The need still remains, as then, for 'people-centred' systems of development worldwide. It is noteworthy that on the day of his death, in his address to an international audience in Switzerland, entitled 'Caring for Real', Schumacher stressed the same theme:

> "Overseas development aid is a process where you collect money from the poor people in rich countries (through taxes) and give it to the rich people in poor countries (through aid)." [1]

Nobody intended this outcome, but it comes from supplying the poor with a pattern of living which only people already rich could take and use. He went on to explain, for the last time, the fundamental error in the industrial societies' perceptions of marginalised people, who need to be treated with respect and dignity despite their poverty.

"The poor are as real as you and me, except that they can do things which you and I can't do; they are survival artists, and it is quite certain that if there should be a real resource crisis, an ecological crisis, a this that or the other crisis in the world, these people will survive. Whether you or I will survive is much more doubtful. You cannot help a person if you yourself don't understand how that person manages to exist at all." [2]

Practical Action

From a basic comprehension of how different communities manage their existence, however inadequately, we ourselves can develop an understanding of how best to help them towards better and more sustainable lifestyles. This has been the consistent approach of the Intermediate Technology Development Group, or Practical Action as it is now called. As it has expanded its outreach in different countries and has gained experience as an organisation over more than 40 years, the charity has experimented with and developed new techniques to meet changing demands. During this time and through a growing number of supporters, it has helped to transform the lives of countless millions of poor people worldwide. Schumacher's thinking has also been a catalyst for change in the approach of other aid donors and development agents working in diversely different conditions and regions. Even global organisations such as the World Bank and IMF are gradually adopting some of these aid policies to support the self-empowerment and resilience of the impoverished regions with which they are involved, despite an ingrained tendency still to offer westernised consultants and overly sophisticated technical solutions.

Even in Schumacher's own lifetime, there were hundreds of examples of where an observation and small intervention by ITDG helped to improve and simplify life at grassroots level – one being the local manufacture of a bicycle with panniers to transport goods to market, together with the setting up of local bicycle maintenance and repair workshops. Another iconic step was the establishment of a highly effective local small-scale egg-tray manufacturing unit in Zambia, to provide safe egg transportation. This was based on a special 'egg-tray template' designed, at Schumacher's request, by Reading University's Department of Applied Engineering. The simple construction, using local materials, proved invaluable for people to be able to carry eggs safely to market over uneven rugged terrain, as previously a vast number of eggs were broken when transported. Practical Action and its partners are today still tackling some of the basic problems of survival by initiating local solutions to specific problems, such as installing solar-powered pumps as well as water catchment devices to give villagers access to clean drinking water. Where there is no means of refrigeration in hot climates, Zeer refrigeration pots, made from local clay, help to store vegetables for much longer periods. 'Floating gardens' allow people to grow crops on top of flood waters: crops are sown on floating bamboo and water hyacinth platforms in flooded regions. Sandbar cropping is another technique. Special seeds suited to specific climate conditions are now being cultivated, propagated and distributed in both flooded and arid regions.

Many other innovative examples are given on Practical Action's website (www.practicalaction.org.uk) and in its publication *Understanding Climate Change Adaptation*.[3] By working with simple and sustainable technologies, Practical Action is now also helping to mitigate the effects of flooding on housing and crops in Bangladesh. At the same time it is looking at ways of diversifying livelihood in Kenya, where it is assisting pastoralists in coping with problems of drought and desertification by producing specific types of seed suitable for tree cultivation and animal fodder. By training local community members, working with schools and local authorities, and by helping to set up project management committees, the organisation strives to ensure the long-term sustainability of all these initiatives.

Practical Action currently employs some 700 people with offices in 13 countries. It works in many regions and countries of the developing world, including Bangladesh, East Africa, Latin America, Nepal, South Asia, Southern Africa and Sudan. The scope of the work has widened considerably in recent years, and communication of solutions and data has been greatly enhanced by the revolution in information technology. In East Africa, for example, projects are being undertaken in agriculture and pastoralism, small-scale manufacturing, transport, urban livelihoods, shelter and renewable-energy generation.

By demonstrating results, sharing knowledge and communicating with others, the culture of development through self-help and community empowerment expands. Practical Action's organisation and its co-workers continue to be inspired by the shared belief that technical change drives wider changes in economic, social, cultural and political life and not vice versa, and that all development must be people-centred.

Today the terms 'intermediate' or 'appropriate' technology still refer to a technical 'middle way', but they also embrace other supportive means by which technical change enables people with few resources to work their own way out of poverty. Thus, in addition to a certain level of mechanisation, the work has come to include accessing an appropriate physical infrastructure, the associated knowledge and skills, and the capacity to organise and use all of these within a cohesive framework – all essential aspects of sustainable development.

According to Simon Trace, Practical Action's current Chief Executive, Fritz Schumacher's influence on the work of this organisation still extends deeply into the core values behind what it does. In particular, the charity has been working increasingly with numerous communities already affected by the early stages of climate change – for example, women and men struggling against the accelerating intensity and frequency of flooding in South Asia, and of drought and crop failure in East Africa. Some of the local solutions devised to meet specific challenges, such as protecting crops and livelihoods against the effects of climate change, are ingenious and can be easily adapted and replicated in other regions suffering similar problems.

The unintentional side-effects of the growth model of development, however, are not limited to climate change. As in Schumacher's time, the model continues to try to justify the 'trickle-down' theory – that the benefits of growth will percolate naturally down to the poorer levels of society such that rich and poor alike will prosper. However, the figures for poor people's access to the most basic services in the developing world bear testament to decades of failure of this approach to tackle poverty at its roots. There are now 1.2 billion people without safe drinking water; three billion without access to safe sanitation; one billion urban slum dwellers without basic housing; and three billion still using wood or dung as their only energy source for heating and cooking. Given this failure, it is extraordinarily disappointing to note the major donor agencies' continued inability to make any radical movement away from the 'trickle-down' approach.

'Right livelihood'

Practical Action continues to put community livelihoods very much at the centre of all its policies. It is introducing and encouraging the use of technologies which can help protect existing livelihoods for poor people in the face of growing environmental stress, and which can help foster the development of small and medium-sized enterprises to create new opportunities for employment. It is also encouraging and enabling the provision of basic services (water, sanitation, renewable energy, housing, transport etc), not just from the point of view of improving access, but also in terms of the role they can play in creating new jobs, both in the local provision of the services themselves and in their productive use. In all of this, sustainability concerns (social, financial and environmental) remain central, as do principles of participation and the idea of enabling people to be in control of their own lives.

As previously outlined, in order to establish 'right livelihoods' Schumacher believed that technologies were needed that were human in scale and which could be owned, understood and managed by those who used them. He also argued for a theory of economics that put the creation of employment at its heart. Technology has to consider the cost of establishing each new workplace as more important than a crude calculation merely of the productivity of each worker. These ideas still remain at the centre of Practical Action's approach to technology. From a financial and social sustainability perspective, poor communities must have the right of choice over technologies which affect their lives, and also the technical capability to operate and control these for their own benefit.

Schumacher consistently argued that we need to rethink our ideas of economies of scale. He was not naïve in assuming that all technology had to be small, but rather he maintained that we should not presume that large-scale was always preferable to small-scale. He seemed almost exasperated at times that people failed to grasp the 'duality of human requirement' in terms of scale. People all need to organise themselves and their structures on a personal and community scale, as well as to understand the national and global dimensions and implications. There is still a constant need to explore new possibilities in each situation and to ensure that decisions are always taken at the appropriate level, from the global to the local.

Outreach

Practical Action works at district, national and international levels to advocate government and donor policies which will bring greater security, more equitable access to markets, and provide other basic services for the poor. It continues to reach out beyond its own projects and beyond the countries in which it has its own programmes, to ensure that the lessons learned from its work and experience can impact on the way other organisations use technology and aid to help eradicate poverty. One outreach method to extend this positive impact is by evaluating and commenting on the opportunities and threats that are posed to poor people by both existing and new technologies. Another effective method is by disseminating knowledge and information, and by responding to requests for advice beyond the boundaries of its designated programmes. This is done through the Technical Enquiry Service (Practical Answers), its consulting arm (Practical Action Consulting), and also its publishing company (Practical Action Publications). 'Small World – Striving for a Better World' is a regular newsletter for friends and supporters of the charity, which is constantly looking for new forms of outreach in an increasingly divided and vulnerable world.

A re-emphasis on small-scale mixed agricultural production for local consumption will remain vital, not just for creating employment, but also for maintaining genetic diversity and combating some of the global issues confronting humanity now. It is also essential to fight climate change, to avoid a future meltdown of our food supplies through disease or pest attack, and to tackle some of the major human health issues caused by the emerging global diet and industrialisation of the food supply chain.

Simon Trace still holds the view that "Practical Action aims to think small in a big way, and demonstrate clearly that these approaches provide a viable pathway to a sustainable and meaningful future for all humanity."

Jeevika Trust, Schumacher Centre for Development and other partners[4]

Alongside the outreach of Practical Action is the work of the Jeevika Trust, which operates exclusively in India. In both organisations the ethos and approach is similar – which is hardly surprising, since both organisations were originally set up by Schumacher, albeit under different names. As he ruefully observed:

> "The starting point for all our considerations is poverty, or rather a degree of poverty which means misery and degrades and stultifies the human person."

Unfortunately, Schumacher's insights about poverty in rural India are still applicable, since under globalisation policies the gulf between rich and poor continues to widen in most developing countries. His proposed solutions, sometimes regarded as prescriptive or unmodern, were driven both by humanity, common sense and an awareness of what was possible in terms of long-term sustainability.

The wider political and economic context in India

In the years following India's independence, Prime Minister Nehru (who had initially invited Schumacher to Delhi to seek his advice) chose to follow a policy of centralised state socialism in line with the dominant political beliefs at that time. Faced with the enormity of the economic task before him, he quickly surmised that realistically there was little chance of inventing and deploying a more decentralised, longer-term, Gandhian approach to rural poverty as advocated by Schumacher. Nehru was not about to be diverted from his commitment to national self-reliance fuelled by government-led industrialisation and modernisation. On the other hand, there were inherent limits to the power of central government to get things done in rural India, and it was somewhat simplistic to see more funding and material aid alone as the obvious and only way to help the rural poor.

Gandhi's advocacy, developed by Schumacher, of 'production by the masses instead of mass production' as the right way forward for sustainability, appeared too revolutionary for Nehru. Schumacher's concepts of intermediate technology were still too far ahead of their time to be taken seriously. Indeed, until quite recently, in the top circles of Indian government Schumacher's ideas were derided as being patronising and even utopian. Intoxicated with the material progress of the elite and the burgeoning middle class, by the attention of the global media and by the technological revolution (from science to information technology), the Indian government puts its energy into promoting global business and still has little time or cause to look backwards at the needs of the rural poor. By contrast, Schumacher believed that development "must reach down to the heartland of poverty" and that "really helpful things will not be done from the centre".

India is a fast-growing economy, and Western commerce is fearful of the Chindia (China + India) economic threat. Yet in both countries there are millions of people without food, work or the basic necessities of life. Despite its accelerating GDP, the need to reduce poverty in both countries is still overwhelming. India has the highest number of people in a single country (300 million) who are below the poverty line. There are another 350 million Indians who cannot read and write; and there are hundreds of thousands of women who die in childbirth because of poor access to health care. Poverty is on the increase despite the growth in the central economy. India's central government, with its focus on global markets, is still unable to provide effective solutions to rural problems. Fortunately Schumacher's approach is at last being vindicated within the new development discourse – investing in renewable energy, water harvesting, small-scale farming, protecting the environment and creating more decentralised development models.

Appropriate technology development

Failing to influence the Indian government's official programme, in 1966 Schumacher decided to set up a rural development organisation in Lucknow – the Appropriate Technology Development Association (ATDA).[5] He relied heavily on the help of George McRobie and also Surur and Mansur Hoda, two Indian brothers whose families came from Lucknow and whom he had come to know in the UK. In the same year, together with George McRobie and Surur Hoda, he set up the India Development Group (IDG), based in London, to raise public awareness and funding to support the work of ATDA. For some years these ventures had an impact, but on a fairly limited scale since funding was always a problem. After the death of Schumacher, and eventually that of both Hoda brothers, the twin organisations were floundering. In 2003 the trustees of ATDA decided to move its head office to Delhi and to rename it Schumacher Centre for Development (SCD), and the London-based IDG became the Jeevika Trust. Under the new leadership of Andrew Redpath, a former trustee of IDG with long-term connections with India, the enhanced organisation has pursued a deliberate Schumacher-oriented strategic direction.

Jeevika is currently engaged in devising strategies and raising funds and support for its various Indian partnership projects, including those of its sister organisation, SCD. These grassroots initiatives focus mainly on water and sanitation; skills training, particularly for women; local income generation; and health and nutrition – all priorities of poor marginalised communities. The funding is mainly generated by members and friends of the Trust (55%), with the rest made up from grants from other trusts and institutions, fundraising events and a small amount of investment income.

Water harvesting and sanitation

As in Schumacher's time, access to safe drinking water and sanitation is still lacking in many regions although they are the most necessary prerequisites for survival. Village-level rainwater harvesting was effectively practised for centuries all over India, but traditional techniques have fallen into disuse and the problem has been widely neglected by central water authorities for two or three decades. The traditional water collection methods differ according to local conditions. They range from wide catchment areas channelling monsoon rain into open reservoirs, where it lies for a while before filtering below ground for access via wells, through to individual roof-catchment kits which enable families and schools to collect and store clean rainwater for household and sanitation use over a period of months. Many of the channels, reservoirs and wells have fallen into disuse or disrepair, and supply is now more precarious than ever. Where the need for them is established, Jeevika's projects offer methods of restoration or the introduction of other water catchment solutions, each being adapted to the local conditions.

For every 1,000 children born in rural India, 87 die before their fifth birthday, mostly from preventable diseases like diarrhoea. Where water harvesting techniques have been applied to village households, community centres and schools, hygiene practices are simultaneously promoted and latrines are built. A successful local water catchment project can not only lead to sanitation facilities and better hygiene levels but also liberate women's time and energy from walking for miles to collect household water. Freed from this chore, they can now be more profitably engaged in income generation activities for their families.

Nutrition

Sound nutrition is another area critical to family health in which Jeevika and its partners are involved. The cultivation of herbs and the establishment of individual 'kitchen gardens', with the help of seed-kits and hand tools, can provide regular vitamins for the family. Home-consumption of honey and, in many areas, goats' milk, can add valuable dietary elements. Extra income derived from honey-production or goat-rearing enables other healthier food ingredients to be bought.

Micro-credit and income generation

As had been experienced by Schumacher, helping poor people lift themselves out of economic poverty still needs much more than foreign aid grants or day-wages from government 'employment guarantee' schemes. The primary need is for skills, collective enterprise, and micro-loans to get started on the process of savings, reinvestment and sustainable income generation. Jeevika and all its partners are active in supporting these different initiatives. It is now well-known that women's Self-Help Groups (SHGs), which have been proliferating all over India in the past decade, have opened up a limitless opportunity for building family security through better nutrition, clothing and literacy. Women in SHGs no longer depend totally on their menfolk, and have proved collectively to have a powerful voice in village affairs, as well as an excellent record of repaying their micro-loans.

Unlike IDG, which raised money only in support of ATDA in India, Jeevika currently works with six other grassroots NGOs. All of these new partners have strong links to the disadvantaged Scheduled Caste, Tribal, and Dalit (previously 'Untouchable') village communities and with women's groups in particular. All are engaged in livelihood projects which assist women's income generation, access to safe water and help for families living with victims of leprosy, HIV and AIDS. The improvements to household income in turn assist improved nutrition, food security, health and hygiene. Jeevika's new partners are described below.

The Schumacher Centre for Development (SCD)

This organisation is now based in Delhi and carries the mantle of the original work set up by Schumacher, McRobie and the Hoda brothers in Lucknow. Circumstances and conditions have greatly changed, but the need among India's rural poor is sadly increasing.

The Schumacher Centre, with its many projects and activities, is currently run by an extremely gifted and versatile Director, Dr Giri. He and other members of staff have built up a network of villagers, volunteers, funders, other NGOs and government officials to address rural poverty and to create opportunities for people to live with dignity and freedom from hunger, deprivation and marginalisation. Its mission continues to be to tackle the roots of poverty in India by embracing Fritz Schumacher's wider concepts of economic development. These include not merely funding projects, but livelihood generation and social change through revitalising rural communities, promoting inclusive sustainable developments, and by sharing the knowledge and use of appropriate technology and local resources.

SCD sees 'livelihood' as an integrative concept embracing education, health, hygiene, human and civil rights, risk limitation and reduction, housing, clothing, skills development, access to means of production, social acceptance and inclusion, and the right to information. In many respects the lifestyles of poor communities in India are worse now than when Schumacher first visited, owing to an increased population, the ever-increasing size of mega cities with vast numbers of slum dwellers, ever-increasing industrialisation and the devastating effects of globalisation on rural areas.

SCD is now mainly engaged in sourcing projects, liaising with different development partners, raising funds, organising training and advocacy programmes, and networking across many different levels. Most of the funding comes from projects and consultancies as well as from the Jeevika Trust. It also has four fully-fledged field offices in the states of Uttarakhand, Madhya Pradesh, Orissa and Tamil Nadu. The field offices are responsible for the direct implementation of projects, although the field staff – full-time, part-time and volunteers – are currently only around 40 in number. However, as the organisation is small and flexible it can apply its resources directly to areas where there is the greatest need, or respond to emergencies. For example in the case of the 2004 tsunami Dr Giri was suddenly able to divert staff and funding to the far south of India to organise a mobile hospital which treated 12,000 casualties within two months. There followed a further project to repair 100 fishing boats, thus restoring the livelihoods to over 3,000 people living in stricken fishing communities.

Social Change and Development (SCAD)

SCAD, a charity based in the Tirunelveli District of Tamil Nadu, is the largest of the new partners. The organisation works in over 450 villages in south Tamil Nadu with the most disadvantaged Scheduled Caste and Tribal community groups, particularly women, and other marginalised groups such as the elderly, orphaned children, gypsies, leprosy patients, snake catchers and people with disabilities. It oversees more than 2,500 Women's Self-Help Groups, currently benefiting a total of about 420,000 women. Jeevika's pilot project with SCAD was to secure the restoration of three traditional water catchment systems, or *ooranies*. These now provide direct village access for over 6,000 villagers to household and livestock water supplies, and have significantly reduced the water-carrying load of women. Again, the initial research and lessons learned have been of great value to Jeevika in planning to expand this type of work in other regions where water harvesting is a priority.

Annai Mary Foundation (AMF)

AMF is located in the Madurai District of Tamil Nadu and since 1996 has developed links with over 60 villages to benefit disadvantaged rural women, particularly Dalit and Tribal women, through various livelihood initiatives. It has built a system of village crèches which provide childcare and enable women to work to earn a living. Jeevika's pilot project with AMF has successfully introduced organised bee-keeping through women's Self-Help Groups, along with the establishment of kitchen gardens supported also by AMF's experience of vermi-composting. All these current initiatives are very much in the Schumacher tradition.

Jeevan Rekha Parishad (JRP)

JRP is based in Bhubaneshwar in Orissa, and since 1992 has developed activities with tribal communities in 25 villages in the Chandaka

Forest area and over 60 villages in the Chilika Lagoon area. It has also helped communities in 10 urban slums. Jeevika's pilot project with JRP was again based on the introduction of organised bee-keeping, supplemented by JRP's own initiatives in developing kitchen gardens. Alongside these projects, JRP has researched the water problems faced by several villages, and has jointly developed four projects with Jeevika to secure the restoration of safe water supplies.

HIV/AIDS

Jeevika's projects also involve providing socio-economic support to families infected with AIDS, as well as building community centres and workshops to provide a shared space for HIV/AIDS families to generate income safely. They are helped to live in sanitary conditions, to look after their children, and are assisted with transport to medical centres for tests and prescriptions. This is an area in which Schumacher was never engaged, as it only came into prominence after his death.

Mithra Foundation (Mithra)

Mithra is located in Tiruchirapalli (Trichy) in Tamil Nadu. Since 1999 the Foundation has implemented health, income-generation and educational initiatives for some of the most disadvantaged village groups in over 80 villages in the Trichy and Cuddalore districts. Mithra has also undertaken pioneering work to identify and meet the needs of villagers living with HIV/AIDS, and to provide socio-economic support for them. Jeevika's partnership project with Mithra has directly benefited over 125 families previously ostracised by HIV/AIDS infection, providing craft space and family facilities, and generating valuable lessons of how to expand and replicate such projects elsewhere.

A tripartite approach to development

In addition to the foregoing, many different levels of problem still need to be explored and addressed in providing sustainable livelihoods for impoverished and illiterate people – from tools and training, to linking products to markets and, above all, joining up with other available support systems. These examples embody Schumacher's tripartite approach to development – linking local communities with help from NGOs, government organisations and businesses.

In most cases, government needs to identify an NGO as a facilitator in the initial phases of development; as a social mobiliser to form collectives; and also to deal with other social aspects such as gender issues. Access to raw materials is still a major issue, as is a lack of a basic infrastructure in many regions. Government also needs to facilitate certain rural developments with the necessary legislative mandate, such as a recent Forest Rights Act in India which transfers ownership to the landless tribals who use forest lands for habitation and farming. Access to finance is another problem: banks will not lend money to the poor and landless without guarantors, so micro-finance credit schemes through self-help groups (SHGs) is the currently preferred route. Micro-finance, in turn, needs necessarily to be linked to micro-enterprise as otherwise recovery is difficult. For better market opportunities, guaranteed quality is another issue, as is an adequate and reliable volume of production to provide for wider markets.

Schumacher pointed out the need for all these sectors to become involved in rural development: he termed it the ABC Principle – administrators, businessmen and communications. In practice, this tripartite approach also requires training and empowering the villagers to organise themselves and helping them to move from development to entrepreneurship mode. The process needs constant facilitation and monitoring at local government level, as well as by NGOs. Women play an integral part as they are the bedrock of family livelihood throughout all poor communities.

Fair trade and accessible markets

For rural producers, finding a fair-trade outlet and accessible market is a big concern. As Practical Action have found, the collection, storage and transportation of goods and produce are also problems in villages where there is little infrastructure. Petty traders and middlemen exploit these weaknesses and pay unfair prices unless the villagers are facilitated by social entrepreneurs. Their role lies in ensuring links to markets at fair-trade prices with guaranteed orders from traders; this is frequently enabled by involving another NGO as a facilitator.

These Third World development issues need to be addressed urgently, systematically and simultaneously. The small-scale approaches outlined in this chapter provide only limited beacons of hope when we consider the magnitude of the problems that are faced. Their value lies in the fact that they all demonstrate local low-cost solutions to local problems, and that they can easily be adapted and replicated in the millions of poor communities all over the developing world. There are now, thankfully, thousands of such initiatives in progress, but there also needs to be much more appropriate input by local NGOs, government, international aid agencies and the commercial sector. The examples cited are because of their direct link with the early initiatives of Fritz Schumacher and his friends, and today with some members of the Schumacher Circle.

Chapter 4

Food, agriculture and land use

"Among natural resources, the greatest, unquestionably, is the land. Study how a society uses its land and you can come to some pretty reliable conclusions as to what its future will be." – E. F. Schumacher

Fritz Schumacher's wartime experiences and subsequent trips to developing countries led to his conclusion that the land is our most valuable *material* resource and not merely an economic commodity. The soil underpins our entire life-support system and is a source of continuous wonder in its constant ability to produce, nourish, sustain and regenerate.

He firmly believed that each country or region should be as self-sufficient as possible, especially in the fields of energy and food production. It should feed its own citizens before growing cash crops for export. Not only does the local cultivation of a wide range of organic, indigenous crops increase food security and reduce transport and packaging costs, but today this is even more significant as a factor in reducing our global carbon footprint.

In addition to his own attempts to cultivate and experiment with an organic garden at his home in Surrey in England (not altogether successful, owing to intermittent lecture tours and overseas assignments), Schumacher constantly quoted Gandhi's exhortation that every able person should participate in some form of physical activity or 'bread labour'. Working with the land offers a unique opportunity for this. Today people are again becoming increasingly involved with organic agriculture, horticulture and food production in allotments or small town gardens. This is seemingly not only for economic reasons and the threat of food scarcity, but to fulfil a deep psychological need to reconnect with nature and to express their own creativity.

However, as world population figures increase, the demand for land intensifies. There is now an unwelcome trend for wealthy individuals, corporations and governments with capital to buy up land from poorer countries for mineral extraction, forest felling, or ethanol production as an oil substitute, and also for agricultural development for the export market and to feed their own populations at home. The Chinese government is ahead of the field in this, now owning large tracts of land in Africa, Latin America and in other regions of the Far East.

Schumacher had close links with many different types of industry worldwide, but he vehemently opposed the Mansholt Plan[1] which treated agriculture as yet another branch of industry, and a fairly inefficient one at that. He never missed an opportunity to point to the fundamental flaw in this agro-industry concept: agriculture and cultivation deal with living organisms, whilst most branches of industry are concerned with inanimate materials. Furthermore, for him, agriculture should fulfil at least three tasks:

To put people in touch with living nature; to ennoble and enrich the wider habitat; and "to bring forth foodstuffs and other materials which are needed for a becoming life". It should, he argued, be the aim of those who manage the land to be orientated towards these three goals. "A fourth goal – the only one accepted by the experts – productivity, will then be attained almost as a by-product".[2]

Today most farmers, whether organic practitioners or from those reliant on chemical inputs, would regard these views of land stewardship as verging on the romantically unrealistic. Competition from imports, unsympathetic government policies and harsh economic realities are currently destroying the livelihoods of many of these food producers.

As custodians of the land and of the heritage of future generations, as well as producers of food, farmers' contribution to society is far greater than the balance-sheet alone. Their work towards securing healthy long-term sustainability needs due acknowledgement and support from government and other sectors of civil society. It is an unfortunate fact that at present, many farmers receive prices for their produce which barely cover their costs, as terms are set by the super-markets which compete to procure food as cheaply as possible. As a consequence, when farmers are forced out of business, the traditions of land management and agricultural wisdom are also lost, and communities become ever more dependent on food imports.

Given both the metaphysical and the practical aspects of Schumacher's thinking and experience, it is not difficult to see why he chose to publicly support the cause of organic farming. These traditional and sustainable agricultural methods had fallen into abeyance in the UK, with the expanding petrochemical industry providing in the short-term plentiful fuel, fertiliser and pesticide products from cheap oil imports. For Schumacher, the use of chemicals and artificial hormones to increase yields in farming did not conform to his lifelong pursuit of non-violence in all walks of life. He well knew that many chemicals successfully kill off weeds, remove blight and improve short-term yields. He was also aware that they destroy millions of micro-organisms essential to the health and fertility of the topsoil, at the same time destroying the delicate and subtle balancing mechanisms of nature. In turn, farmers become dependent on external industries to supply artificial nutrients and defences for their crops which could otherwise be achieved through traditional land management systems. In the long-term, soil quality becomes degraded and crop yield diminished.

Space only permits a few examples of ways in which Schumacher's personal convictions about sustainable patterns of agriculture have directly influenced thinking in this field today.

The Soil Association

The UK Soil Association was founded in 1946 by a group of far-sighted farmers, scientists and nutritionists, headed by Lady Eve Balfour, who became its first President. These visionaries saw that environmental health lay in making the connections between good farming practice and health. At the time their main focus was on scientific research and experiment. Despite an impossibly overloaded diary, Fritz Schumacher became very interested in this research, and was later honoured to be associated with the work of the Soil Association when in 1972, Lady Balfour invited him to become President.

Lady Balfour believed that the simple recipe for health lay in connecting the organic links in the food chain between soil, plant, animal and man. Herbicide treatments in pastures and drugs administered to animals quickly find their way into the human bloodstream and other organs, and are gradually proving a long-term health hazard. Schumacher, when President of the Soil Association, also concluded that chemicals in the food chain must eventually have an impact on human health, and that insufficient scientific research had been dedicated to this aspect.

It has also since been scientifically demonstrated by numerous research establishments, including the Quality Low Input Food Project,[3] that, whilst inorganic compounds may initially enhance crop production and animal productivity, the long-term effects are detrimental to the entire food chain. Various studies and reports concur that there are significant differences in the beneficial mineral, vitamin and trace element levels which are consistently lower in crops treated with inorganic products. This, in turn, has a negative impact on human and animal health – hence the growing market in vitamin and mineral food supplements. The topsoil also loses its resilience to disease and its ability to retain moisture, which makes it more likely to be washed away through flooding. In arid regions this significantly reduces crop yields and increases the risk of gradual desertification.

As early as 1971, when addressing the Soil Association's 25th Anniversary Conference, Schumacher had spoken of the need for the organic movement to be forward-looking and always to keep up to date with its aims, methods and research. The Soil Association, he urged, should "continue systemic work on the system of wholeness" – soil, plant, animal, man. He suggested, however, reversing the order. "The knowledge of what you do with the soil is limited to farmers and a few others. Twenty-five years ago we could say we begin with the soil; now we might say we begin with man and trace it back to the roots, because unless we cure the sickness in the roots, expenditure on the National Health Service will continue to rise and will achieve nothing." This unfortunately continues to be relevant today.

Schumacher also stressed the need for the Association to "reach out and enthuse, as well as to act as custodians of the organic tradition". He urged that it should present its research to a much wider audience, engage young people in its ideas and find new patterns of co-operation with other organisations to spread its essential message more effectively. "We must make our message into a story . . . Right ideas, in order to become effective, must be brought down and incarnated in this world".[4] This message is still reflected in the Soil Association's policies and outreach, and is proving very relevant. The 'storytelling' needs to embrace a new generation for very many obviously practical reasons.

Peter Segger is a co-founder of Organic Farm Foods and an active Board Member of the Soil Association. Writing from Blaencamel Farm in Wales, Peter pays a personal tribute to his former friend and mentor. "We were total amateurs in growing and in understanding organic techniques, but we were keen and idealistic. Fritz Schumacher looked around our weed-covered fields and simply oozed encouragement, support and guidance, with great touches of humour and inspiration. One always stayed with me: asked why he always used the Biodynamic methods for sowing seeds, he replied pragmatically that this took the burden of decision-making from him. 'Just follow the calendar and it will work. It reduces the need for yet another series of decisions to be made – simpler!!' We were so new to growing vegetables that it was just the lift we needed."

Schumacher was President of the Soil Association at a time when finances were in dire straits and when staff relations could have been very much better. Peter Segger says that "he infused a new spirit into the Association and led it into a whole new world where the young new organicists were now strongly enthused by his articles, lectures and his total generosity in donating the royalties of his world best-seller, *Small is Beautiful*, to our deeply depleted cash reserves." He also says that Schumacher had persuaded the UK Government to take over the management and reclamation of an open-cast coal mine at Bryngwyn in west Wales, where difficult, degraded soils were eventually converted to fertile land – including the very productive organic farm where Peter Segger now lives.

Since its faltering early days the Soil Association has become the UK's main organic organisation. It is increasingly well-known for its certification scheme and the logo which verifies over 70% of the organic food, drink, textiles and cosmetics sold in the UK. The aim of setting up the organic standards scheme was to define and audit sustainable farming practice so that the public could trust certified goods as being authentically organic. Its standards are now amongst the highest in the world, and the Association currently validates and licenses over 2,800 UK organic producers and 1,200 food processors. To become certified, producers must avoid the use of all chemical fertilisers and pesticides, introduce fertility-building crop rotations and adopt management practices which promote positive health in plants and animals (thus benefiting the human species also). Food processors also must adopt similarly stringent codes of practice concerning food additives.

The work of the Soil Association also covers a wide range of educational activities which are becoming increasingly important. These include promoting more nutritious school meals from local organically sourced food; developing the highest farm and animal welfare standards; and encouraging sustainable and fair trade food policies at all levels. The UK media has become increasingly involved in these campaigns with various health, culinary and gardening gurus rallying food producers, as well as the public, to adopt organic production and consumption patterns.

Patrick Holden, director of the Soil Association 1995-2010, and his team brought the work of this vibrant educational, campaigning and research organisation very much into the 21st century, greatly increasing its scope and membership as well as stressing the mitigating contribution of organic farming to reducing the global carbon footprint. Helen Browning, who succeeded him, is also firmly committed to bringing organic food into the mainstream, and continuing to encourage the public to purchase directly from the producer through the expansion of box schemes and farmers' markets. This not only benefits farmers and reduces overall costs, but also has an added beneficial environmental impact in terms of decreased packaging, storage and transport.

Organic farming, based on a combination of traditional practices and current research, needs to be demystified and made more readily available to the public. Practical information packs, literature and guidance for new enthusiasts are obtainable directly from the Soil Association. Its quarterly members' magazine *Living Earth* is a further source of organic growers' news, research findings, exchange and information.[5]

The Transition Towns Movement

Started in 2004/5 by Rob Hopkins in Kinsale, Ireland, and now based in Totnes in Devon, this movement has the aim of providing local solutions to respond to the interrelated problems of peak oil and climate change. 'Transition' has quietly been spreading from its base to many distant parts of the globe, including Canada, Australia, New Zealand, the USA, Italy, Brazil and Chile. There are now over 380 designated 'transition initiatives' worldwide and Rob Hopkins' primer, *The Transition Handbook*, has been translated into over nine languages.[6]

The concept of Transition is derived to a considerable degree from the principles of permaculture, based on Bill Mollison's seminal book *Permaculture: a Designer's Manual* (1988) and David Holmgren's *Permaculture: Principles and Pathways Beyond Sustainability*. It is a current exemplar of Schumacher's thinking in practice, not only by supporting community agriculture and local sales of produce, but by building community resilience to future oil and food shortages in times of crisis. It is also a very practical means of reducing our carbon footprint and combatting global warming.

The way in which each community tackles its 'transition' varies from place to place depending on local conditions and culture, and the energy and ambitions of the people involved. The initiatives vary widely between localities (which in some places includes setting up their own local currency), but most have in common the aim of reducing carbon emissions by the reduction of food miles, cutting unnecessary transport and waste at all levels, and encouraging local, organic food production and community sharing schemes.

Schumacher's holistic vision of agriculture was inevitably also connected with his views on community health, security and the economics of permanence. With the interrelated food and fuel shortages experienced today, this enthusiasm for organic, community-based, agricultural production systems is still relevant, particularly in industrial countries.

Silviculture

Closely connected with his promotion of organic agriculture was Fritz Schumacher's enthusiasm for saving indigenous forests and for 'forest farming' and the planting of fruit- or food-bearing trees, sometimes as 'three-dimensional crops'. With proper local knowledge and appropriate soil and climate conditions, certain trees are capable of yielding food, animal fodder and also medicinal and chemical compounds. They can provide building materials and biomass fuels from residues, whilst sometimes sheltering secondary crops planted underneath. As a friend of Richard St Barbe Baker,[7] Schumacher personally encouraged tree-planting schemes wherever he went, pointing to the fact that the real value of a tree lies in the many functions it performs whilst living and growing, whereas most accountants and economists only regard its value in terms of cash for timber or pulp once it is felled. Sadly, even the landmark UN Conference on Biodiversity held in Cancun in 2010 (COP16), failed to secure any binding international agreements on preserving primal forests and international woodlands, and the destruction of forests for short-term commercial gain continues apace.

A growing number of diversely different organisations worldwide are nevertheless actively engaged in silviculture, forest farming and agroforestry. Others are supporting or establishing schemes for the protection of woodlands and forests in their own districts to help to counteract the devastating climatic effects of logging and deforestation by gigantic industrial concerns elsewhere. One notable example is the work of **Tree Aid**. This Bristol-based charity, founded on Schumacher's development principles, is successfully demonstrating today the multifarious benefits and practical tradable products derived from their tree-planting projects in many poverty-stricken, arid and formerly barren regions of Africa primarily in Ethiopia, the Sahel and Burkina Faso.[8] However, it seems unlikely that these local schemes can possibly keep pace with the rate of destruction without international legislation on forest protection. Tree-planting is at last being recognised as a prerequisite for establishing soil protection and rural livelihoods in some of the very poorest regions of the world.

Third World

Schumacher was always indignant at attempts to convert Third World countries into abandoning their diversified traditional agricultural methods, and adopting the use of imported chemical fertilisers and pesticides in order to supply monoculture cash crops to the industrial world. Their subsequent history of debt, dependency, loss of biodiversity and soil fertility and the ensuing crop vulnerability is a testimony to how this message has so far failed. Many Third World peasant farmers, having changed from their traditional agricultural methods, are unable to pay the mounting costs of the chemical inputs on which they have become reliant and, in desperation, have committed suicide. Moreover, countless genetically modified (GM) crops which they have planted have produced a constellation of problems: when the crops have failed there is no recompense from the suppliers; contrary to the company's assurances, the crops have needed expensive pesticides; and because the GM varieties contain the 'terminator' technology, seeds cannot be saved from year to year.

Other hazards encountered by farmers – even in the rich countries – are when the crops of organic cultivars are contaminated by chemical drift from adjoining land which has been treated with inorganic compounds or by GM crops. GM and nanotechnology crops are often grown experimentally without public knowledge, acceptance, or without reference to possible long-term environmental implications. In the case of GM organisms, contamination is usually permanent – once 'the genie is out of the bottle' it cannot be recaptured. Moreover, GM crops have so far not been shown to produce consistent or better yields, although they can be pest- or drought-resistant. They are also designed to destroy the ability of the plants to reproduce themselves, and thus deplete nature's sustainably diversified seed banks. To achieve this, GM seeds have sometimes initially been supplied free by multinational producers to poor farmers to lure them onto the treadmill of having to purchase future seeds instead of harvesting and saving them from their own traditional crops.

Fortunately there are countless thousands of individual organic growers and organisations worldwide who are now fighting back against the giant corporate food monopolies. The growing organic movement in India is an encouraging example. In certain areas the peasant farmers have had the courage to maintain their traditional and organic methods in the face of relentless pressures from industry, government and other external agencies, often in the face of financial incentives, personal setbacks and daunting economic uncertainties.

Organic farming methods require knowledge, time and patience. They involve embracing a fairly uncompromising system of organic composting, spreading manure and other natural mineral compounds on the land and adhering to systematic crop rotation to enhance soil fertility and to build up communities of bacteria, fungi, flora and fauna in the soil. Any interruption by chemical intervention to such a programme can have serious consequences and it is therefore necessary to adopt a long-term time frame, which is not always acceptable to farmers who wish to see a quick return on their investment.

The International Coalition
to Protect the Polish Countryside (ICPPC)

Another current example of Schumacher's thinking in practice in a very different agricultural context comes from Sir Julian Rose, President of the International Coalition to Protect the Polish Countryside, which was established by Jadwiga Lopata in 2000. Julian was formerly on the Council of the Schumacher Society UK, a board member of the Soil Association, and also runs a pioneering organic farm in South Oxfordshire.

The mission of the Polish Coalition is to demonstrate that it is still possible to live by the fruits of the land without destroying either the landscape or the soil, and without losing the social, spiritual and cultural community links that form the bedrock of a healthy society.

Currently partly living in Poland, Julian vigorously campaigns to protect local small farmers from being coerced into amalgamating into much larger farms and adopting the industrialisation of agriculture promoted by the European Union, of which Poland is now a member. He speaks with both authority and passion on the validity of Schumacher's approach in the traditional agricultural communities of the European Union today.

"Schumacher, as we have seen, was profoundly aware of the contribution that exponents of traditional mixed rotational farming practices made to the long-term health and welfare of both soil and society as a whole. The great majority of government and corporate institutions, however, have failed to share such enthusiasm for local solutions to global problems. The spread of 'big' technical agricultural developments is extolled as the panacea for today's food, energy and fuel needs and frequently encouraged by hefty subsidies, largely unknown to the taxpayers." [9]

In the case of Poland and other EU countries, genetically modified crops and large-scale agrochemical farm-intensification programmes to supply hypermarket chains are purported to be the modern way forward to bring their farming in line with Europe's Common Agricultural Policy. To quote Julian Rose:

"The result will be to prise Poland out of its long-established self-suffi-ciency pattern of family farming, and to place her assets at the disposal of the global marketplace with its cut-throat commercial exploitation and blatant disregard for community solidarity."

The ICPPC and its supporters contend that if one works effectively at the local level, where authorities still have some direct connection with the land and community, it is possible eventually to influence national government policy even today. Rose comments that Schumacher's views on land use are still relevant:

"Schumacher was highly effective in influencing influencers at the local and regional level, something that was particularly apparent during excursions to India and Africa. In Poland, rather than adopt-ing strategies (often with financial incentives to farmers) of corporate monoculture conformity, the European Union, as well as the various national and regional governments, would now find it more socially and economically efficient to embrace some of Schumacher's eminently practical and compassionate approaches to integrated community land and energy management projects."

Other connected initiatives

Many different organic agricultural projects exist which are closely con-nected with Schumacher's legacy. Fritjof Capra's Center for Ecoliteracy [10] in California and Vandana Shiva's Navdanya project [11] in Dehra Dun, India, are two noteworthy examples which extend the outreach of the growing educational movement for local organic agriculture and nutritious food production, and both have close connections with Schumacher's thinking. Both centres provide practical education and training, and serve as research and demonstration models. As Vandana Shiva writes, "We can and must respond creatively to the triple crisis (global warming, peak oil and the resulting food crisis) caused also by globalisation of the rights of the poor to food and livelihood, with the triple opportunity to reinvent society, technology and economy." [12]

Conclusion

In April 2008, after a four-year study by 430 scientists from all over the world, the International Assessment of Agricultural Science and Technology for Development (IAASTD), under the chairmanship of the UK's Professor Bob Watson, delivered the first ever assessment of global agriculture. Unwittingly, it was a validation of Fritz Schumacher's thinking. Their report concluded that organic agriculture can simultaneously contribute to delivering global food security, help tackle climate change, protect soils and conserve wildlife. It also criticised industrial agriculture for being 'too narrowly focused' and called for a move to more holistic farming systems which aid both biodiversity and local communities. In the words of Bob Watson, "business as usual is no longer an option". He also questioned claims by the GM lobby that GM crops provided a solution to global poverty, hunger or climate change and concluded that there needs to be a global shift to 'agroecological' food production.[13]

Successive UK governments' overt support of the GM industry is well-known, despite mounting scientific evidence demonstrating that it is neither cost-efficient nor particularly productive, so the way ahead is not altogether promising. Although the 'Precautionary Principle' has not yet been enshrined in UK law, Schumacher was always adamant that adequate scientific research should be undertaken before any new substance or chemical agent was introduced into the food chain, atmosphere or water supply. His whole philosophy towards agriculture was one of uniting experimentation and innovative thinking with traditional wisdom, precaution and humility, being ever vigilant of the 'Law of Unintended Consequences'.

Chapter 5

Small-scale technologies for local sustainability

The Centre for Alternative Technology

"The concept of efficiency has become quite narrow and exclusive: it relates to the material side of things and only to profit." – E. F. Schumacher

The Centre for Alternative Technology

Long before the discovery of oil in the North Sea in 1969, Schumacher warned against industry's increasing dependence on this fuel source, mainly imported from the politically volatile regions of the Middle East. He saw that increased energy efficiency and the development of renewable resources had great potential to reduce our political and economic energy vulnerability. Then came the 1973 oil crisis, which coincided with the publication of *Small is Beautiful*. Although the policy of industry and government was to resume 'business as usual' as soon as possible, many forward-thinking people began to doubt the sustainability of the consumer society. Their questioning, in turn, gave birth to numerous experiments in local self-sufficiency, one of which was the Centre for Alternative Technology (CAT). Gerard Morgan-Grenville, a very active and imaginative environmentalist and social entrepreneur,[1] much influenced by Fritz Schumacher, decided to set up a pioneering community centre in an abandoned slate quarry in mid Wales at Machynlleth. Its unique purpose was to test, and demonstrate to the public, the efficiency and effectiveness of different types of devices that harnessed renewable energy.

In 1974 the first pioneers moved in to start building a purposeful community. This was designated the national Centre for Alternative Technology (CAT).[2] In the words of Peter Harper, who first coined the term 'Alternative Technology', and is currently Head of Research and Innovation at the Centre, "It was originally intended to be a kind of ark for technical knowledge and skills in the event of widespread social breakdown." It has since become a thriving community whose mission is to develop and demonstrate all kinds of methods of self-reliance and sustainability.

Peter reminds us that in those days some sort of global societal or financial collapse was widely expected "either through nuclear war, the Marxist revolution or ecological implosion. . . . In radical and environmental circles, apocalyptic thinking was then quite common!" This thinking called for a different kind of post-industrial technology. The logic was that after social or economic collapse, people would have to rely on local materials and components which they could obtain within the region or make themselves. The concept provided a direct link with Schumacher's thinking for developing countries, since it aimed to create resilience against failures in the supply chain or lack of an effective infrastructure.

Although the expected catastrophic crisis appears to have been somewhat delayed, our industrial society is now definitely entering an era of enforced transition for completely different reasons, which range from the effects of global warming to the pressures of an exploding world population and widespread shortages of basic commodities. During what is likely to be a period of growing turbulence in all walks of life, the lessons learned at CAT will be increasingly relevant to Western society, as local self-reliance becomes more and more necessary.

Even in the early days there were many direct parallels between the work being undertaken at CAT, and at Schumacher's Intermediate Technology Development Group and also at the Appropriate Technology Development Association in India. There was a regular exchange of information with ITDG, joint participation in courses, and some collaboration in the training of VSO volunteers.

CAT's main work has evolved in many different areas, some of which reflect the spirit of Schumacher's direct or indirect legacy.

Renewable energy technologies

The development of renewable energy technologies is still CAT's main mission. In its early days Schumacher had been delighted to find that in the UK an organisation was actually addressing this subject so close to his own interests, and which he had been promoting in Third World countries through ITDG. At CAT, full use has been made of all the available ambient energy resources – sun, wind, water, ground heat, and biomass – for both heating and electricity generation. The diversity of modern models now on display at the Centre, Harper claims, "are mostly benign and hard to abuse. Their intrinsic limits tend to keep things in proportion. No business enterprise could corner the market in solar or wind energy as they might in oil or uranium."

In the mid-1980s the entire site ran on just a few kilowatts, and was wholly independent of the grid. However, to maintain consistency of supply required clever juggling on the part of the resident engineers and also draconian load-control. In 1990, after much argument within the community, it was decided that grid-linking was the way forward because it allowed small generators to contribute efficiently and to use the grid as a kind of storage battery. It also allowed something approaching a 'normal' supply, in expectation that eventually the future would be an all-renewable grid-based system. Such a system might include electricity exports and imports and to and from Europe, with millions of large and small feed-in generators. This has yet to be achieved. Although the UK now has 'feed-in tariffs' (FITs), and other financial incentives, these are somewhat less attractive than those of many other European countries and domestic renewable energy systems are developing less rapidly here than elsewhere.

The electricity system at CAT has evolved steadily, although the supply has often struggled to keep up with the growth of demand as the organisation has expanded. 2008 saw the installation of a combined heat and power (CHP) plant using local wood chips as the main source of energy. This small-scale CHP system is still in its experimental stages and one of CAT's engineers is conducting leading research in this much-needed field of technology ideally suited to communities, schools and hospitals. In addition there is 7kW of water power available and up to 20kW of solar-generated electricity. CAT still expects to be a net exporter of electricity into the grid in the foreseeable future.

Low-energy buildings

Although energy generation is CAT's best-known activity, its experimentation with heat conservation in buildings is probably more successful and important. A typical modern building uses 80%-90% high-carbon industrial products in construction with 'garnishes' of traditional materials. At CAT the aim is to reverse this ratio, with 80% or so of local materials such as wood, earth, straw, slate, stone, paper, wool and lime, and only 10%-20% of 'industrial vitamins' (mostly membranes, adhesives, fixings and glass) that have to be acquired from elsewhere.

The buildings are all designed to use very little energy in operation, and to be healthy for the occupants, well-lit and flexible in use. The Centre's most recent project is the opening of a £7 million Welsh Institute for Sustainable Education (WISE) complex, which is designed to be the greenest building in Wales. Its performance is currently being monitored very carefully. WISE uses rammed earth, timber frames, and a relatively new material, hemcrete. Hemcrete consists of a mixture of hemp fibres and hydrated lime that is either used in blocks or sprayed onto walls. This gives excellent sound and heat insulation using a zero-carbon material.

Water and wastes

Although no longer so driven by the notion of total 'self-sufficiency' as in the 1970s, in many areas CAT has actually achieved a sustainable model. Water for all purposes (hydropower, irrigation, washing and drinking) is provided from a stream-fed reservoir above the site, inherited from the nineteenth-century slate workings. Drinking water is cleaned by slow-sand filters (a classic intermediate technology device) and ultraviolet light (a good example of non-chemical treatment suitable for medium-scale supply). After use, the waste water is all cleaned on site with no energy or chemical inputs – using just gravity, plumbing and plants. The Centre has also created advanced designs for waterless toilets which will be of great benefit in the forthcoming age of water shortages, as well as to community sanitary schemes in Third World countries.

Food wastes were originally processed by feeding them to pigs and poultry, an efficient system for generating high-quality protein and useful manure. Sadly, the current Animal By-Products Regulations no longer allow this, and a large proprietary machine had to be installed. It is, in effect, 'a mechanical pig', but with nothing edible produced and inferior 'manure'. The Centre's view is that this retrograde and uneconomical step has been taken solely to comply with the constantly changing food production regulations and is detrimental to the cause of long-term sustainability.

Organic food production

From the outset CAT has adopted an 'ultra-organic' approach to its food production, using no agrochemicals whatsoever. One result is that pest problems (apart from slugs!) have been negligible. The Centre has also been able to demonstrate the immense potential of soils for sequestering carbon through the regular incorporation of organic material. An unexpected side-effect has been a far higher biological diversity than that of the surrounding farmland, despite the rapid development and intense human activity on the site itself.

Organisation and finance

On the organisational side, CAT's structure has evolved gradually with the general aim of striking a balance between efficiency and democracy. It is, in effect, a social enterprise owned by its permanent members, who also constitute the responsible management, overseen by a committee of local trustees. The Centre is intended to be a model of how an organisation of any kind, whether a residential community, a campaigning body, or a business enterprise, can be self-governing and flourish by adapting to changing circumstances. In the words of Peter Harper, "One imagines that Schumacher would have appreciated the evolution of a system that can cope flexibly with rapid growth and maintain the essential principles of self-management."

Volunteers

Alongside its permanent staff and community members, CAT still attracts many volunteers, whose hard work and skills are essential to the running of the organisation. They, in turn, further their own skills and environmental knowledge, and in due course use them to benefit a wide variety of organisations which cover a range of disciplines: from engineering to ecological architecture, to organic agriculture and teaching.

Research

CAT has also evolved as a centre for research at many different levels. However, if there are facts to discover or new systems to develop, the community tries to focus primarily on the problems encountered by householders rather than on commercial operations. It employs a simple low-tech, practical, interdisciplinary style of research, relating specifically to the kinds of topic chosen.

Some examples of key research areas are simplified home-composting methods and improved containers; the incorporation of solar photovoltaics as part of a building's structure; testing the strength and thermal properties of composite building materials made from natural products; using a mixture of greywater and urine to simultaneously fertilise and irrigate crops; and also researching methods of cleaning waste water under different conditions. Research projects sometimes generate useful income through grants, and at the same time the knowledge gained feeds back into CAT's other work and publications.

Education and training

The fastest-growing sector of the Centre's work is education and training. Courses for the general public were started in 1979, and today CAT offers about 60 a year covering an extremely wide variety of topics. As well as the more usual 'Community Renewable Energy Systems', 'Gardening for a Sustainable Future' and 'Convert Your Engine to Vegetable Oil', there is 'Teaching Sustainable Development and Global Citizenship', the annual 'Sustainable Science Symposium' and 'Humanity and Nature: A Spiritual Exploration'.

In recent years the explosive growth in CAT's activities has been in higher education. There had always been visits from university groups, but early in the present decade one of the London universities suggested CAT run a 'semi-distance-learning' MSc course in sustainable architecture, where the students would attend the Centre for one week per month. This was immediately successful, and the numbers have virtually doubled each succeeding year. The Centre now has several hundred registered postgraduate students on what has become the largest masters course in sustainable architecture in the UK. Its popularity seems to result from the unique combination of high-quality classroom teaching and hands-on practical work. The WISE building was purposely constructed to meet these new demands, but already is appearing too small for the growing numbers of applicants. A new department, the Graduate School of the Environment, has recently been planned, and a further MSc in renewable energy has been added, with other courses in progress. There are already several PhD students at CAT which is steadily evolving into a type of do-it-yourself micro-university.

Visitor demonstration and information facilities

The most immediately visible aspects of CAT are the tourist/visitor demonstration facilities, with the usual car park, toilets, restaurant, shop and information points. The Centre attracts about 60,000 'drop-in' visitors a year, mostly in the summer, but the same facilities can be used for courses or training during the low-season.

The on-site shop is open all-year round, selling a large range of 'green' books and products, and it has a successful mail order operation. The Centre also has its own publishing company with 100 titles currently in print, ranging from one-page 'tipsheets' to full-colour textbooks.

There is a free information service available to inquirers via post, phone, email, or in person. In recognition of its public value, the information service is largely funded by grants, but it also generates business for other departments. Where inquirers need more comprehensive information or guidance, there is a paid consultancy service. The most common requests are for help on eco-buildings, renewable energy, organic waste and water treatment, and also on eco-tourism.

A catalyst for local regeneration

CAT has 'spun off' several daughter companies, including Aber Instruments[3] (located on the science park in Aberystwyth, making electronic equipment), and Dulas Engineering[4] which specialises in technology for developing countries, mostly connected with remote energy systems. Numerous other enterprises and activities in the area almost certainly would not exist but for the historical presence of the Centre and the new markets it has created. CAT was also instrumental in the setting up of Ecodyfi,[5] the sustainable development agency for the Dyfi Valley region. Ecodyfi has, in turn, stimulated all manner of new initiatives. This is perhaps the most striking example of the spirit of Intermediate Technology: dozens of small enterprises and other organisations being generated, mostly providing environmental and social 'products'. Although wages in the region remain modest, hundreds of meaningful jobs have been created and the regeneration is far more strongly-rooted and 'robust' than with the typical development initiatives imposed from outside.

According to Peter Harper, although it has taken the Community and its supporters 37 years to get to this point, the reputation of the Dyfi Valley as the sustainable dynamo of Wales "can be traced back to the small group of dedicated people who started CAT, and were proud to acknowledge the inspiration of E. F. Schumacher."

CAT is still clearly a trailblazer, opening up ever new opportunities for putting concepts of sustainability into practice. Its ongoing development provides a tangible demonstration of certain aspects of Fritz Schumacher's thinking about local energy generation and sustainable communities, but many other similarly interesting experiments and examples exist. These range from Amory and Hunter Lovins' Rocky Mountain Institute[6] in Colorado to the Findhorn Foundation[7] in Inverness and to The Eden Project[8] in Cornwall, to name but a few. All have direct or indirect links with Fritz Schumacher's vision of sustainability and, as such, provide practical and educational exemplars of his legacy today.

The importance for the future is to study the experiments and lessons of these various demonstration models, and to see how and where methods of reducing our own energy demand and environmental impact can be applied within our households and communities as we face the combined environmental pressures and energy shortages of the 21st century.

Although all these projects happen to be based in industrial countries, there are now many similar initiatives in developing regions. The transfer of technology, technical training and information is now of paramount importance if we are to meet the challenges ahead.

Chapter 6

The call for a new economics
nef and the E. F. Schumacher Society

"In the current vocabulary of condemnation there are few words as final and conclusive as 'uneconomic'. If an activity has been branded as uneconomic, its right to existence is not merely questioned, but energetically denied." – E. F. Schumacher

By profession Fritz Schumacher was an economist, albeit a highly unconventional one. During his early years and career he had been exposed to many different aspects of the 'science' of economics. It was primarily during his 20 years as Economics Adviser to the National Coal Board and later as its Director of Statistics that Schumacher gained many experiences and insights into the workings of government, industry and economic attitudes in both developed and Third World countries. These led him to challenge some of the most basic assumptions about the way in which conventional economics was applied at all levels.

One aspect of economics which dismayed Schumacher was the narrowness of its interpretation in the West. A paper called 'Economics in a Buddhist Country', which he wrote as early as 1955 (after a brief secondment as Economic Adviser to the Burmese government), expresses his misgivings.

"All life has an economic aspect......so we must all be economists or materialists or good householders. But one thing is surprising, and is indeed abnormal, namely that there should be only one 'science', only one body of thought, called Economics. What today is looked upon as the science of Economics is based on one particular outlook on life, the outlook of the materialist. Economics distinguishes between 'productive'

and 'unproductive' activities, and only those are called productive which in one way or another, directly or indirectly, cater for material wants."

Many of our contemporary economic thinkers, such as Hazel Henderson, James Robertson, Wolfgang Sachs, Amory Lovins, Bill McKibben and Molly Scott Cato, have since expanded on this theme. The voluntary sector, or 'meta-economy', makes an essential and often unrecognised economic contribution to society's wellbeing. The informal roles of caring, cooking, cleaning, mentoring, child-rearing and so forth – which are usually undertaken by women, family members or neighbours and sometimes called 'the love economy' – are now increasingly acknowledged, although their input can never be monetised and measured in terms of productivity.

There is also a welcome new tendency to examine some of the wider social and environmental implications of corporate and government economic policy in terms of these broader definitions of economics. Yet the old narrow materialist view is deeply ingrained, despite all the evidence as to its malfunctioning and inherent limitations. One aspect has, however, dramatically changed: there is now a groundswell of media- and NGO-led public opinion which is challenging the current economic model. It is the thousands of 'little people', and those without great wealth or authority, who are coming together in demanding more just, fair and equitable economic policies. They form societies and pressure groups to campaign for an environmentally safer world which is not measured only in terms of economic productivity. Schumacher's vision of economics went well beyond these.

In the early 1970s, being ever more disillusioned with the narrowness and exploitative nature of most contemporary economic thinking, Schumacher pleaded passionately for a "nobler economics that is not afraid to discuss spirit and conscience, moral purpose and the meaning of life, an economics that aims to educate and elevate people".[1] After his retirement from his 'office job' at the National Coal Board, he set about exploring and testing out some of these wider aspects of economics with various different organisations and audiences. His visionary proposals on the subject have given rise to a great many think-tanks and alternative experiments around the world. For the purposes of this Briefing, we will focus on just one or two initiatives which have a direct link to his thinking.

The New Economics Foundation

The New Economics Foundation (**nef**) was founded in 1986 by the leaders of the first and second TOES (The Other Economic Summit) Conferences. The aim of TOES had been to challenge the international economic agenda set by the original G7, a club of the world's richest nations then meeting in London, and to pursue some of the wider social and environmental implications of *Small is Beautiful*. **nef** set about exploring the practical alternatives to the materialistic and centralised norms of Western economic thinking – hence its own subtitle 'economics as if people and the planet mattered'. It now sees itself as a 'think and do tank': working within communities to create change from the grassroots up, as well as striving to change 'ideas, policies and institutions' at the highest level through its research, publications and communications work, mainly with government bodies and other public organisations.

The original intention of **nef** was also to take forward the thinking of Schumacher and others in the field of economic policy. Its twelve founding members and trustees were from different walks of life but unanimous in the realisation that an economic system targeted on growth was hopelessly ill-equipped to solve the pressing and inter-related challenges of environmental damage, growing inequality and social injustice. Humanity urgently needed to shift to a radically different kind of economy: one whose primary goals were to increase individual and collective well-being, based on the sustainable use of resources and social justice.

The need today is for an economics closer to the meaning of 'oikos' (Greek for 'household') from which the noun stems: one where our children and grandchildren can share a planet whose environment is flourishing rather than approaching catastrophe. There is a need to create a system where inequality is dramatically decreased rather than constantly growing, and where human and environmental health and well-being are continuously improving.

Paul Ekins, nef's first director, wrote in 1986 in his preface to *The Living Economy* (based on papers from the two earlier TOES events in London)[2] that new initiatives "will continue to develop and campaign for a sane, humane and ecological new economics". nef's task is now "to bring together the new economic ideas which were surfacing throughout the 1970s and sporadically before, and place them within a coherent, consistent theoretical framework, which would facilitate their comprehensive promotion and further development". Step by step, this is gradually being realised.

After 25 years, new systems and economic institutions are still needed: institutions founded on clear ethical principles and operating within the limits of environmental sustainability. In some respects nef has made significant headway, and other organisations have also taken up various aspects of its cause. Today nef also explores many related areas not directly addressed by Schumacher himself, such as banking reform, monetary reform, local currency initiatives and ethical procurement policies and guidelines, as well as the various well-being indicators.

As Stewart Wallis, nef's current Executive Director, wrote in his Foreword to *From the Ashes of the Crash*:

> *"A new economic order is emerging. This is a genuinely historic – and for many painful – time. But it presents us with a unique opportunity to build a financial infrastructure that actually does the job that the old order failed to do: to value and protect our social and natural operating systems. In a new economy, these are what must be valued and invested in: not the hollow, unsustainable and destructive premises of easy credit, consumerism and unsustainable economic growth. A return to 'business as usual' is not an option."* [3]

In practical terms, in the years since its foundation nef has built up a coherent body of theory, research and practice around the new economics. These have begun to direct and inform regional and government policies as well as many grassroots communities. Its practical tools for change are gradually taking root in different organisations and institutions, both in the UK and internationally. Its ideas and campaigns have also helped to bring about a shift in public attitudes and assumptions across many areas, and have in some instances changed government policies which, in turn, have benefited the lives of millions of people.

Small is Beautiful brought together for the first time many of the central ideas which remain at the heart of nef's thinking to this day, namely:

- that the economy is part of a wider framework, the 'meta-economy', and that economic decision-making needs to take into account social and environmental impacts. Again, as Stewart Wallis puts it, "We believe that we cannot keep growing the global economy indefinitely when we are now coming up against clear planetary limits. The economy is a subset of the ecosystem." [4]

- that small is not only beautiful, but resilient in the midst of the powerful forces of globalisation. With the growth of giant transnational companies and the erosion of local life, and with the majority of those in developed countries utterly dependent on unsustainably cheap global transport for even basic necessities, people are increasingly looking to stronger local communities with local and regional economies as the place where resilience and sustainability are to be found;

- that work plays a pivotal role in the life of individuals, families and communities, and goes far beyond the narrow economic model of paid work, and that 'good work' (or 'right livelihood') is a major contributing factor to well-being;

- that economics does not exist in an ethical vacuum despite the evident assumption of many in today's financial and banking sectors. As Schumacher maintained, *"No economic doctrine or theory stands on its own feet: but it is invariably built on a metaphysical foundation – a person's basic outlook on life, its meaning and its purpose."*

- that living well does not have to cost the earth, and a life lived within environmental limits is likely to make people more rather than less happy. 'Well-being' research, as pioneered by **nef**, shows statistically what most people have always felt intuitively: that companionship, family, purpose in life and time to reflect, are more important to living a fulfilled, flourishing and happy life than money and material goods.

The meta-economy

Schumacher and others have noted how conventional economic accounting fails to consider the central importance of social and environmental goods upon which the global economy relies, and which he termed the 'meta-economy'. Decisions made without reference to this wider meta-economy, although they may seem to add up within the confines of a narrower economic framework, frequently have repercussions which are catastrophic in the long term to both environmental and human well-being. **nef**'s work on the 'core economy', further develops this idea, focusing on the economy of human and social assets.

Governments' relentless pursuit of GDP as the defining measurement of progress has proved exceptionally misleading. One needs only to look at circumstances which are disastrous for the environment and human well-being but result in increased GDP to be aware of its basic limitations. War, for example, is a GDP success story. In her book *The Shock Doctrine*,[5] the economist Naomi Klein argues in detail that disasters and catastrophes, as witnessed by the past three decades, are not only highly profitable but essential for maintaining the power of the politically elite. 'Disaster capitalism' as she calls it, enables politicians to pass legislation which would otherwise be highly unpopular, undemocratic or economically questionable. Pertinent examples are the ever-increasing anti-terrorist legislation; or the financial crises which enable governments to transfer public wealth and social services into private hands in the name of urgent economic expediency. In a 'crisis', everything is assumed to be politically legitimate or economically necessary. The link between increased GDP and increases in people's well-being is in fact weak after a certain (relatively low) standard of living is reached.

Since 1994 **nef** has been developing alternative indicators to GDP, with its first *UK Index of Sustainable Economic Well-being* (ISEW) produced for the Foundation and the Stockholm Environment Institute by Tim Jackson and Nic Marks.

The indicators are based on consumer spending, but incorporating positive and negative adjustments to account for environmental, health and social factors. These include habitat loss, depletion of non-renewable resources, the effects of climate change and the costs associated with crime and unequal income distribution. Well-being takes into account health, life expectancy, social and cultural factors and ecological footprints rather than merely GDP and consumption levels. This is very much in line with Schumacher's contention that a person or community's well-being cannot be measured in economic terms alone.

Happiness and well-being

Since 2001 **nef** has worked actively in promoting well-being as a legitimate aim of government policy, and has developed a wide range of tools and publications that help to incorporate social, environmental and other relevant factors into economic decision-making. This is now beginning to take root in government planning. The *Happy Planet Index*,[6] first launched in 2006, brings together the environmental footprint and human well-being in a single measurement by showing how efficient countries are in converting their natural resources into long, fulfilling lives for their citizens. A new Centre for Well-Being was created at **nef**'s London office to facilitate its pioneering work in this area. The Centre conducts research and consultancy to promote well-being as a policy focus at local, national and international levels. It has developed robust and valid measures of well-being for policy-makers, organisations, communities and individuals, which have been adopted worldwide as valid indicators of true economic success.

In 2009 **nef** launched the 'National Accounts of Well-being: bringing real wealth onto the balance sheet',[7] aimed at getting this important concept to replace the 'growth' measurement in government initiatives. In its small publication *Are You Happy?* it points out that if the whole world were to share the UK's lifestyle we would need over three planets, and that overconsumption of resources is not making rich countries happier. The UK, in fact, which has the 18th biggest ecological footprint in the world, only comes in 108th place in the Happy Planet Index. The G8 countries, as a whole, score very badly, whereas many island communities such as Malta appear to enjoy much higher levels of well-being. All this detailed research demonstrates what many suspect – that increased wealth does not guarantee increased happiness. People can, in fact, consume less and experience greater well-being for themselves and their environment.

Green New Deal

In July 2007 **nef** published another important work: the *Green New Deal*,[8] on behalf of the Green New Deal Group. Britain was facing a 'triple crunch', (the combination of a credit-fuelled financial crisis, accelerating climate change, and soaring oil prices underpinned by peak oil production). The Group came together to develop strategies and to explore ways in which this threefold crisis could be tackled in a holistic way as well as creating new jobs to revive the economy. The ideas and language of the *Green New Deal* report have been taken up in varying degrees by the UN, the US, Japanese, South Korean, Irish and UK governments. **nef**'s work in this field continues to develop and expand despite the daunting enormity of the tasks ahead.

Social return on investment (SROI)

The development of **nef**'s Social Return on Investment (SROI) is another measurement tool demonstrating how organisations and policy-makers can incorporate social, environmental and well-being returns into economic decision-making, and has already been applied to a range of public policy areas. **nef** has also worked with the Office of the Third Sector as part of a consortium to refine and standardise the methodology so that SROI can be used throughout government in the UK. In effect it provides a means to integrate Schumacher's theory of 'meta-economics' into public policy decisions. Many other examples exist of tools and methodologies which **nef** has developed for incorporating social and environmental factors into economic decision-making within the public and private sector, including nef's sustainable commissioning and sustainable procurement models.

Global interdependence

Fritz Schumacher was concerned by the fragility of our dependence on multi-layered and long-distance connections. He commented that as everything and everybody had become mobile, all structures were threatened and vulnerable to an extent never known before. Partly in response nef has set up an Interdependence Day and produced *The UK Interdependence Report*,[9] both of which acknowledge our material interdependence on the environment and on each other. They highlight the perversity of 'ecologically wasteful trade', whereby every year thousands of tonnes of virtually identical goods are traded between countries. Global interdependence has only been possible because the low cost of transport has not reflected the true, long-term cost of fossil fuels or costs in terms of environmental damage. There is also an ecological debt day. This is the date in a calendar year when the UK, if it were dependent solely on its own natural resources, would completely exhaust them for the rest of the year. In a globally interdependent world, it becomes the day when the UK begins to live off the resources of the rest of the world having used up its own. That date is falling earlier each year (in 2010 it was 21st August), which should give us all considerable cause for concern.

Connected economies

A large part of nef's recent work has involved helping to make local economies and local communities more resilient, and protecting the diversity and character of local life. *Plugging the Leaks*[10] is an economic literacy package which enables people to explore together how their local economy works and to develop ideas for improving it by preventing money and assets flowing out of the community. There is obviously also a strong connection here with the Transition Towns Movement mentioned earlier. *The Local Multiplier*[11] is another useful guide which enables local businesses and local government to measure the economic impact of their activities on the local economy and to see how to enhance that impact. This initiative is now being shared internationally, working in partnership with grassroots organisations in Israel, Brazil, South Africa and elsewhere. Their report on 'Clone Town Britain',[12] describing how town and city high streets have been taken over by supermarket chains thus driving out their smaller local competitors, received wide media publicity. The purpose of this initiative was to demonstrate the chain of negative social and economic impacts and to stimulate people to support their local shops and businesses.

Co-production

In *Good Work* Schumacher described how, in conventional economic terms, work is "an item of cost, to be reduced to a minimum if it cannot be eliminated altogether" and hence "the ideal from the point of view of the employer is to have output without employees, and the ideal from the point of view of the employee is to have income without employment."[13]

Many of the elements of Schumacher's vision of 'good work' are brought together in nef's development of the concept of co-production. The premise is that we need to widen our ideas about what constitutes work beyond the narrow definition of 'paid employment'. The new vision includes recognition of the incredibly broad range of social activities which contribute to community life and social networking, and without which the money economy itself would be unable to function. The basic principles of co-production are that it defines every individual as an asset, with something valuable to contribute, and that it recognises the value of reciprocity. In the context of public services, users are viewed not as a drain on resources, but as having a crucial contribution to their effective functioning. nef currently works to promote this approach with many public service organisations and local authorities by providing tools and training, including a co-production audit.[14]

Time banking

The concept of co-production also underpins such innovations as Time Banking and similar reciprocal systems that are based around the community currency of 'time credits'. Originally they were invented in the 1980s by the US civil rights lawyer Edgar Cahn. **nef** developed the idea, set up some of the first time banks in the UK, and founded the London Time Bank and the Time Banks UK networks. These are now both part of a single independent umbrella organisation. Central to the time banking model is that all the participants' time is valued equally: an hour for an hour, whatever a person's qualifications, age, or status. People exchange expertise and services without any money changing hands. There are now over 100 active time banks under the umbrella of Time Banks UK.[15]

Banking and access to finance

The recent global banking crises of 2007-2011 show that banks have become unfit for purpose. Through decades of lax regulation, sector consolidation, lack of transparency and a focus on financial speculation, banks have moved a long way away from their roots as lenders and investors in communities. Many organisations have been working since the early 1990s to redress this balance and to research alternatives. A major tranche of **nef**'s work has been its involvement in the growth of the community development finance sector. **nef**'s input to the UK Government's Social Investment Taskforce in 2000 led directly to the introduction of Community Investment Tax Credits in the 2001 Budget.

In May 2011, three years on from the full outbreak of the banking crisis, the Good Banking Summit was convened by **nef** and Compass. This brought together over 100 experts representing more than 60 organisations to discuss what a reformed banking sector would look like and how it could be achieved. The resulting report, 'Good Banking – Why we need a bigger public debate on financial reform', could be seen as radical by the complacent institutions concerned, but is well worth reading. It is obtainable from **nef** and can also be downloaded.[16]

Community finance and co-operatives

This project aims to reduce the wealth inequalities in the UK (50% of the UK population now owns only 1% of its wealth, whereas a generation ago the figure was 12%). There is a growing movement to support the 5,000 co-operatives and also to lessen the widening gap in pay differential between those at the bottom and top of corporations.[17]

Promoting economic and ethical justice

In the past **nef** has led and supported campaigns against many social and economic injustices, from the irresponsible profits and speculation of the banking system to private loan sharks and doorstep lenders, to lobbying MPs for a Post Office network of 'People's Banks'. It has also published guidelines on Ethical Purchasing,[18] Ethical Trading and been a pioneer on social auditing (its first social audit being The Body Shop in the early 1990s). Experience shows that information and public pressure can effectively help bring about policy change, such as through the Jubilee 2000 movement which was co-founded with **nef**. This campaign put the issue of poor-country debt onto the international agenda and led to billions of dollars of debt cancellation for Third World countries.

Centre for the Future Economy

A Centre for the Future Economy was set up in 2007 at **nef**'s London office to develop a detailed vision of how a more moral economy could and should function in the future, and to build a positive alternative to the current economic system, based on the new economics that is now beginning to emerge around us.

The E. F. Schumacher Society (USA)

No Briefing on the impact of Fritz Schumacher's ideas today would be complete without including our sister organisation in Great Barrington, Massachusetts, USA. This is the centre of another vibrant and expanding network of activists and thinkers in the Schumacher tradition. It was here in the Berkshire Hills that the E. F. Schumacher Society (USA) was founded in 1980 by a group of Schumacher's American friends and colleagues under the leadership of Robert Swann and Susan Witt.[19]

Background

Swann, a lifelong pacifist and Gandhian, had read Schumacher's articles in *Resurgence* and in 1967 went to England to meet him. A great friendship was formed, and in 1974, the year after its UK launch, Swann organised a North American tour for Fritz to promote *Small is Beautiful*. It was at the end of this tour that Schumacher suggested that Swann convene a US-based group of thinkers to work at the interface of economics, land use and applied technology, since these were the subjects of many of their discussions. It was only after Fritz's death, and at the insistence of others, that Swann set up the E. F. Schumacher Society with Susan Witt as the executive director, to fulfil the mission envisioned by Schumacher six years earlier. Robert Swann died in 2003, but Susan remains the inspirational director of a very dedicated team and network of supporters who are working at many different levels, both theoretical and practical.

One eminent supporter is John Fullerton, a former Managing Director of JPMorgan Chase and now a friend and adviser to the Society. He points out that at the theoretical level there is finally a fundamental recognition that today we face two main problems in our economic system. The first is the credit-driven contraction, leaving the entire middle class vulnerable and the poor further distressed and increasingly desperate. This is what has captured the attention of business and financial leaders, politicians, and the mainstream media. The second problem is more profound. We are currently amidst an accelerating conflict, predicted by Schumacher almost 50 years ago, between our growth-driven economic system and the finite limits of the planet. So far, however, we are mostly focused on its symptoms, such as the increased awareness of climate change risk, water shortages, the collapse of whole fisheries, rising raw material prices led by oil, and food scarcities not imagined even a year ago. In short, we are at risk of being distracted by the current stresses in the financial system that overshadow the more profound scale challenges we face. Moreover, in the words of Fullerton:

> *"The linkage between a global interconnected financial system and the real economy seems to loosen during the boom times. Finance spirals higher into increasing abstraction and complexity, with previously unimaginable wealth accruing to the relatively few who control increasingly massive concentrations of capital along the way."*

Unfortunately, many of the remedies for the first problem will inevitably be in conflict with the difficult choices we face in addressing the second problem. On the one hand, stimulating growth is the solution to cyclical downturns, yet on the other hand, more growth of our resource-intensive global economy presses against the known physical limits of the biosphere. Hence the world faces a profound conflict which cannot be ignored. We are trapped in a growth-driven economic system which is collapsing, not because of the credit-crisis, but because the credit system is predicated on perpetual resource-driven growth with no recognition of scale limitations.

Today we are daily witnessing the symptoms of an economic system catering for an ever-growing world population and the finite limits of the natural world. What we are not hearing, at least in the mainstream media, is a critical reframing of the questions that address root causes. Nor are we hearing a debate about the sustainability of a perpetually growing global economic system nested within our finite biosphere. There is no debate about the wisdom of allowing financial power (and risk) to be concentrated in fewer and fewer financial institutions of increasing complexity and scale. Yet we are now all experiencing the results first-hand. What we all need to grasp is that the financial crisis we are reacting to is a mere sideshow to the much more profound challenge we face with respect to the sustainability of our economic system as a whole. The present financial crisis is a wake-up call to this far greater challenge.

To rely on technical solutions alone to solve our sustainability challenges – that are themselves the products of technological advance – is not wise. As Schumacher advocated, we must think more at a meta-physical level in the search for genuine and lasting solutions. Clarifying the first principles of this truth, as effectively as our collective wisdom allows, is our most urgent task. These opening decades of the 21st century may be our best chance to launch the critical transformation of our economic system into an economics of permanence. This has been the quest of the E. F. Schumacher Society over the years.

The Society has taken a four-part approach to implementing Schumacher's vision of a new economy. The first is similar to the UK Schumacher Society, in that it convenes seminal conferences and lectures, which also create an atmosphere of fellowship, celebrate achievements and provide a forum for continuing discussion. The second is to develop an extensive website and printed publications programme, and to collect and archive material at the E. F. Schumacher Library on the theory and history of decentralised economies. This Schumacher library also houses all of Fritz's personal books and papers. The third activity has been to encourage communities to explore ways to renew their local economies. Lastly, the Society has launched a successful local currency. In the current financial climate this initiative has attracted by far the most interest and publicity.

Community Land Trust in the Southern Berkshires

Community Land Trust founder, Bob Swann, believed that at the heart of changing the direction of our current path is a re-evaluation of the way we treat land. The speculative market that has arisen around land ownership is having a threefold effect: denying affordable access, tying up community capital, and limiting local employment. On the other hand, placing land in a community trust excludes the possibility of making a profit from inflating land values. In the absence of this speculative gain, the productive use of land becomes more profitable. When land is no longer viewed as an investment in itself, capital is freed up for other investments. Both of these processes – gaining access to useable land and the freeing of investment capital – serve to create new employment opportunities.

Michael Gordon, Outreach Co-ordinator of the E. F. Schumacher Society, observes that the perception of land changes as a border is drawn around a region of economic activity. What was once merely an object of speculation now becomes a vital and finite resource necessary for the sound economic health of the regional community. Investment priorities shift from holding land for resale and financial gain to using the investment money to develop the land in a beneficial way – for workforce housing, affordable access to farmers, or for attracting new businesses. The freeing of capital from the land creates a vast investment pool for the development of local economies – a key factor in any region of high unemployment. In the Berkshire Hills of western Massachusetts, the Community Land Trust is currently providing an affordable means to home ownership for forty local residents, and land access to farmers who are providing organic food to numerous local families.

SHARE (Self-Help Association for a Regional Economy)

The SHARE programme was a simple way for residents of the Berkshire region to provide micro-loans for the start-up of small businesses. A member of SHARE was able to start a savings account at a participating bank that was opened as a joint account with SHARE. The savings book was used as collateral for a loan that the bank normally would not make, and that in turn made it possible for the borrower to create products needed by the community.

SHARE served the region from 1981 to 1992, and collateralised 23 loans with a 100% rate of repayment. The programme's slogan became, "Do you know what your money is doing tonight?" Gradually the regional banks themselves learned to make the small loans to local businesses once served exclusively by SHARE, the programme was no longer needed. Simple to operate, the system still remains a useful tool for citizens to make loans available to underserved populations. The power of SHARE is that it allows the community to decide what types of business it wants, and it leverages a community's capital to make those businesses possible.

BerkShares

BerkShares are a local paper currency which is tied to the US dollar, and was launched by the E. F. Schumacher Society in 2006 before the recent financial collapse. They are now the biggest alternative cash system in the USA. Printed on special paper by a local business (a subsidiary of Crane Paper Co., which has been printing US dollars since 1879), the currency can only be spent within the Berkshire region. The notes, in denominations of 1, 5, 10, 20 and 50 BerkShares, are purchased from local banks at the rate of $0.95 for one BerkShare, and are used for local transactions in The Berkshires. The vendor may sell BerkShares back to the bank for federal currency at the rate of $0.95 for one BerkShare. Dubbed a "great economic experiment" by the *New York Times*, this local currency has attracted a great deal of media attention both nationally and internationally. By August 2011 there were over 2.7 million BerkShares in circulation, issued through 13 branch offices of local banks, and with approximately 400 regional businesses participating.

BerkShares are a tool for community empowerment, enabling producers, merchants and consumers 'to plant the seeds for an alternative economic future for their own communities'. They require a personal economic exchange, as the citizen/buyer must enter into direct communication with the merchant/producer about the item or service purchased. There is inevitably a growing awareness of the many roles played by various members of the community and of their different businesses and occupations. These small and slow exchanges are countering the abstract tendency of money by reconnecting financial transactions with the people, culture, and landscape of a particular place. At the same time they are gradually building up the community wealth which is the foundation for a newly imagined economic system. To facilitate the wider dissemination of local currency schemes, the E. F. Schumacher Society has produced and updated a local currency directory covering similar schemes which are now emerging all over the USA as they are elsewhere in the world.

Issuing alternative currencies is legal as long as it is treated as taxable income and consists of paper bills rather than coins. However, the growing success of BerkShares in a failed economy has led to the

E. F. Schumacher Society pondering the wider questions, such as who should issue currency, and how it is actually valued. It is becoming more aware of the intricacies of currency issue and how to advocate for sounder, fairer monetary policies at a national level.

The New Economics Institute

A very recent and positive development has been that in 2010 the E.F. Schumacher Society has become the New Economics Institute, working in conjunction with **nef** in the USA.[20] Stewart Wallis, **nef**'s Executive Director, has joined the Board of the New Economics Institute, and in May 2011 they opened an office in New York in order to more easily be able to exchange staff and expertise with **nef**. The goal of the Institute is "to help create a cultural shift simultaneously on both sides of the Atlantic through non-partisan work with business, academics, and policy groups".

The programme of the Institute includes: a continuation of the E. F. Schumacher annual lecture series, organising conferences and seminars, and developing community land trusts and local currencies.

The economics of permanence

As witnessed by his many lectures and writings, Fritz Schumacher foresaw that the various interlinked environmental crises which have now become critical worldwide, are inextricably a part of the international economic crisis. Centralised patterns of production create wealth accumulation for a few, and job loss for many. We now face a financial crisis in which governments fail to account for their debt, and financial institutions collapse from their speculative investment practices, together with a resource crisis as we remove finite substances from the Earth at an increasingly frenzied rate. There is a growing social crisis in which human rights are being systematically abused, and a cultural crisis created by a numbing uniformity of products alienated from the unique history of a people and place.

As an antidote, Schumacher offered a systematic solution based on deeper spiritual values and traditional wisdom. He called for a building of new institutions that follow ecological guidelines, different models for business, worker ownership and participation, affordable access to land, organic farming practices, energy conservation, the use of renewable energy and, above all, cultural restoration and spiritual renewal. In *A Guide for the Perplexed* Schumacher outlined the inner renewal required by citizens to implement these transformations. As we have seen, different organisations have taken on board and combined different aspects or facets of his approach. The E. F. Schumacher Society in America (New Economics Institute) has gradually evolved a systematic approach to tackle many of these interrelated areas simultaneously.

To make the transition from a dominant global economy to a system of co-operating local economies confronts a number of the most pressing issues of today with positive alternatives. The programmes of the E. F. Schumacher Society are providing a new language and framework for this transition. Fritz Schumacher not only included well-being, environmental conservation, social justice, cultural renewal, and appropriate scale in his discussion of economics: he made them the basis of economic health. Again, to quote Michael Gordon,[21] "Schumacher was a prophet of our current interrelated crises and a proponent of what he called 'economies of permanence'. Moving toward these economies requires a coherent strategy that includes both education and action. The programmes of the E. F. Schumacher Society are developing both the fundamental knowledge and the practical applications for building strong regional economies that successfully address the questions raised by ecology, social justice, and resource use."

In the words of John Fullerton, an active supporter of the New Economics Institute:

> *"Schumacher's gift and genius was to derive economic principles and ideas from these [great philosophical and spiritual] teachings; to have the courage to speak the truth, despite knowing it often flew in the face of conventional economic thinking; and to make the truth accessible with his clear and witty prose. What emerges is certainly not the final*

word on the economics of permanence. Some of his thinking is outdated, or simply missed the mark. But as a foundation to build upon, it is invaluable. The reason his ideas about economics ring true is because they are built upon these wisdom traditions. The contradictions of modern economics are gone." [22]

Chapter 7

Transforming industrial work in the First World

"An industry is, in essence, nothing more mysterious than a body of men associated, in various degrees of competition and co-operation, to win their livelihood by providing the community with some service it requires . . . its function is service, its method is association." – E. F. Schumacher

Much has been written about the impact of Fritz Schumacher on the course of economic development in Third World countries. However, little has been publicised about the effect of his thinking on high technology and industry in the developed world, even though he spent 20 years of his working life in the UK's National Coal Board. His legacy in this field has been limited to date, partly because the centralised structures of industrial conglomerates are not particularly sympathetic towards the concept of smaller, more autonomous entities. Moreover, the individual, partly self-reliant units which Schumacher advocated would prove an impediment to the onward march towards globalisation with centralised systems concentrating ever more capital and power in fewer hands, as is the case today.

The Coal Board

In the 1950s and early 1960s, during his time with the National Coal Board, Schumacher had become increasingly concerned about the vulnerability of many large industries, given their centralised structures and dependency on uncertain fossil fuel supplies. However, the subjects on which he was able to develop his thinking were forecasting (as Director of Statistics) and the relationship between coal and the emerging nuclear power industry.

Forecasting

Although a statistician and economist by training, Schumacher frequently warned against the peril of predictions, and from basing future policies on the assumption of past trends continuing on a linear progression. This certainly posed particular difficulties in his field of energy forecasting, and especially for coal, where any significant new development in production plant has a lead time of up to ten years. In the case of nuclear power generation, this can be much longer. Rather than committing future energy policies to forecasts which depend on the interplay of numerous institutional, economic and geo-political factors, he preferred to base them on 'exploratory calculations' which tended to be more flexible and could be adjusted according to current conditions. He stirred controversy when he claimed that "the whole process of detailed forecasting, with all its spurious elaboration, in the end amounts to little more than a roundabout way of asserting 'everything will remain as before, only more so'. The subsequent discovery of oil and gas in the North Sea, eastern Europe, South America and under the oceans, together with the continued instability of the Middle East, have certainly validated this position.

Nuclear power

While Schumacher worked there, the National Coal Board was in open competition with the developing nuclear industry, although most of the hierarchy considered that nuclear power would gradually take over from coal as coal extraction became 'uneconomical'. This was a term Schumacher challenged, arguing that the economic aspect could not be applied to non-renewable resources. Fossil fuel could only be evaluated in the total context of all available energy options at the time and, in the case of nuclear power, the waste storage and decommissioning costs were uncertain and incalculable. This has proved true to this day in that all these actual costs so far have always greatly exceeded budget. The financial deficit is still unknowingly met by taxpayers. Schumacher made a plea for a long-term energy strategy which included all non-polluting energy technologies and especially energy efficiency, advanced solar technology and developing the other renewable options. He strongly advocated immediate investment in energy efficiency equipment at all levels, and in research and development of non-fossil fuel technologies. His emphasis on matching energy generation methods to the most appropriate end-use, introducing energy conservation methods, and reducing energy waste and transmission losses is even more relevant in the 21st century. As he remarked, "What is the use of heating water to 1,000°C if the end use is to use it for washing or bathing at 40°C?"

In October 1967, at the height of the coal versus nuclear debate, in a keynote lecture at the National Society for Clean Air, Schumacher raised a public outcry by voicing doubts about the safety of nuclear reactors and the feasibility of long-term waste containment and storage. Although quoting from over 35 eminent authorities and official reports, he ended on a personal note:

> "The continuation of scientific advances in the direction of ever-increasing violence in nuclear fission and moving to nuclear fusion is a prospect of terror threatening the abolition of men. Yet it is not written in the stars that this must be the direction. There is also a life-giving, life-enhancing possibility, the conscious exploration and cultivation of all relatively non-violent, harmonious, organic methods of co-operating with the enormous, wondrous, incomprehensible system of God-given nature of which we are a part."

During his time at the National Coal Board he became an external consultant to various companies and organisations. He often encouraged these to put aside 5% of their turnover for investment in R&D and 'lifeboats' – complementary alternative approaches to their main products – and to diversify their services in case their current markets were challenged or collapsed. He likened the 'lifeboat principle' to the

Italian ice-cream seller who sold umbrellas from his van during the winter months.

One of the few disappointments felt by Schumacher after the publication of *Small is Beautiful* was the apparent lack of interest in his ideas among most mainstream industrialists and academics of the Western industrial persuasion. For some years he was simply regarded by them as a controversial, clever and entertaining intellectual with interesting but somewhat quirky ideas. Typically, when he was invited to address an audience of business people they would delight in the delivery, but were perplexed as to the content. How, he was often asked, could one apply his doctrine of intermediate technology in a highly complex, international large-scale industrial environment? Surely, from a purely technical point of view, any engineer could demonstrate that it was simply uneconomic to ignore the 'economies of scale'. Also, it was one thing to move from a 'primitive' technology to an 'intermediate' technology, and thence to a 'sophisticated' technology – then both productivity and profits would rise together. But to reverse the order would surely be a retrograde step. There was an uneasy feeling that these ideas implied regression and an abandonment of the concept of progress, rather than a reordering of thinking.

Schumacher's starting point, again, was that of human scale – creating useful and rewarding work employing non-violent technologies in an environment where workers could relate to one another. Inevitably he had difficulty in communicating this message to the captains of industry. Their *raison d'être* was an obligation to their shareholders. Their aim was not to promote fulfilling work, but rather to further and foster faster economic growth underpinned by ever more sophisticated technology. Their obligation was, therefore, to increase productivity and consequently to achieve greater profits as quickly as possible.

In the face of the sudden oil crises and global economic threats of the 1970s, it was hardly surprising that public and political attention should be concentrated on the mainstream concerns of industrialists – economic revival and restoring growth. It was left to a few dedicated individuals to apply Schumacher's ideas on technology to the modern industrial sector.

This divergence of values was also the main reason why, for many years, Schumacher's true disciples in the industrial West were initially to be found among those who had, in fact, already rejected the industrial way of life. Among his early acolytes were the hippies in the 1970s and later the 'Greens' in the 1980s, as well as the more liberal intellectual academics in the universities and certain leading NGOs.

Three areas in particular had always been prominent in Schumacher's writings on work, but have not been followed up with any widespread effect. These were the humanisation of work; ownership and governance; and the encouragement and development of small-scale organisations and sustainable enterprises even within larger national or multinational structures. He had argued that these three strands, if implemented, would lead to a reduction in unemployment and more rewarding work, less human and material wastage, and also create more meaningful jobs. Schumacher believed that small firms – or an appropriately sized department of a larger firm – were crucial to the efficient functioning of the modern company. These smaller units were more flexible in the face of fluctuating demand, provided an outlet for entrepreneurial talent, and were a seedbed for innovation and creativity.

The plight of the unemployed, Schumacher claimed, had to be seen by government as having a negative effect not only on economics, but on family life and on all the related social issues and structures of society. He passionately argued this case during the 1960s in the face of government policy to close the 'uneconomic' coal pits in favour of cheaper coal imports, but was overruled. His ideas on industrial structures were largely ignored by all but a handful of companies with whom he had some form of direct contact or consultancy.

By the arrival of this new millennium, an uneasy feeling has been growing and spreading throughout Western society that 'the party's over'. Ever-increasing size, speed, scientific and technical advances and resource consumption have come up against the physical limits of existence on a finite planet. It is no longer the case of a controversial set of ideas being confined to a few left-wing or liberal intellectuals and out-of-touch ecologists. Many of Schumacher's predictions are now materialising, somehow without conscious recognition. In *Small is Beautiful*, he actually anticipated our current situation:

> *"In the excitement over the unfolding of his scientific and technical powers, modern man has built a system of production that ravishes nature and a type of society that mutilates man. If only there were more and more wealth, everything else, it is thought, would fall into place. Money is considered to be all-powerful . . . The development of production and the acquisition of wealth have thus become the highest goals of the modern world in relation to which all other goals, no matter how much lipservice may still be paid to them, have come to take second place. The highest goals require no justification; all secondary goals have finally to justify themselves in terms of the service their attainment renders to the attainment of the highest. . . .*
>
> *This is the philosophy of materialism, and it is this philosophy – or metaphysic – which is now being challenged by events. There has never been a time, in any society in any part of the world, without its sages and teachers to challenge materialism and plead for a different order of priorities. . . . Today, however, this message reaches us not solely from the sages and saints but from the actual course of physical events. It speaks to us in the language of terrorism, genocide, breakdown, pollution, exhaustion."* [1]

The humanisation of work

The humanisation of work, or 'technology with a human face', as Schumacher called it, was a recurring theme in many of his writings and public addresses.

> *"Considering the centrality of work in human life, one might have expected that every textbook on economics, sociology, politics and related subjects would present a theory of work as one of the foundation stones for all further expositions. . . . However, the truth of the matter is that we look in vain for any presentations of theories of work in these textbooks. The question of what the work does to the worker is hardly ever asked."* [2]

Today the work situation in industrial countries is changing rapidly, partly due to a growing awareness of Corporate Social Responsibility (CSR), stemming from the human relations departments within industry itself, and partly instigated by the trade unions. There have been many valiant attempts to democratise and emancipate companies' own work-forces and to extend their legal rights. Numerous academic and socio-logical research reports have since been published on the effects of work and work conditions on workers, their families and their communities, so many of Schumacher's criticisms in this respect have been addressed.

In his later years, Schumacher himself was rapidly developing his own understanding of the various options available to the designers of modern industrial equipment and machinery. These included the relative merits of automation; appropriate-scale advanced technologies; different meth-ods of assembly; computerisation and so on; and their consequential effects on the welfare of the worker. Despite his background in econom-ics, philosophy, theology and Third World development, his somewhat overloaded work and travel schedule tended to curtail the time he had to follow up new research. His personal interest in the engineering aspects of industrial work was only aroused towards the very end of his life and was never followed up, even though the effects of new technological developments were always of great personal interest to him.

Ownership and governance: The Scott Bader Commonwealth

In principle Schumacher was a supporter of co-operatives, having stud-ied a number of attempts to build a moral way of operating in business as opposed to the mere 'profits and power' principle that is still preva-lent today. For a great number of years his mind had been occupied with the question of ownership, social justice in work organisations, employee rights and participation in a company's decision-making pro-cesses, and in a fair and just distribution of profits.

At the time when he was grappling with the above issues, Schumacher had the good fortune to meet with certain people who were to act as catalysts to his thinking on the structure of ownership. One such was Ernest Bader, the founder and owner of the Scott Bader Commonwealth, whose Board he joined in 1965. The case history below is given in some detail as it demonstrates a completely innovative pattern of ownership in which Fritz Schumacher became enthusiastically involved. Although it seems not to have been replicated, it still serves as a useful blueprint which could be adapted and adopted by any number of different companies today.

Ernest Bader was Swiss, and had emigrated to England. In 1920 at the age of 30 he had started to sell Swiss celluloid, and this led to him setting up a pigment paste manufacturing company in London. By 1951 Scott Bader Co. Ltd. which, during the war, had been evacuated to Northamptonshire, had become a highly successful and prosperous medium-sized family business employing 161 people. The company was now a product leader, producing polyester resins and other substances such as alkyds, polymers and plasticisers. Yet as a young man with a deep conscience, Ernest had disliked the depersonalised concept of 'employees', 'a labour market' and a 'wages system', particularly because he disliked a system where capital employs humans rather than humans employing capital.

As he was a Quaker in the position of a successful employer, and the family had sufficient income to re-evaluate their lives, Bader wanted to make some revolutionary changes in the way industry was based, and to avoid sowing 'seeds of violence'. He believed that the family company should reflect a philosophy which attempted to fit industry to human needs, and not vice versa.

> "I realised that – as years ago when I took the plunge and ceased to be an employee – I was up against the capitalist philosophy of dividing people into the managed on the one hand, and those that manage on the other. The real obstacle, however, was Company Law, with its provisions for dictatorial powers of shareholders and the hierarchy of management they control."[3]

The problem was how to reorganise Scott Bader Co. Ltd. to give people a maximum sense of freedom and involvement without loss of profitability; and how to do this by ways and means generally acceptable to the private sector of industry. These were exactly the issues which Schumacher had been deliberating. It soon became apparent that for such radical transformations there needed to be not only profit-sharing, which Bader had practised from the very start, but a complete transferral of ownership to the workforce. In addition, Ernest himself needed to give up some of his managerial controls of the Company or, in his own words, undertake "the voluntary acceptance of certain self-denying ordinances".

The first step was taken in 1951, when Ernest Bader transferred 90 percent of the ownership of his firm to the workforce and formed the Scott Bader Commonwealth. In fact it was not until twelve years later, and after much profound deliberation by the founder and shareholders, that the final ten percent of the family's ownership was transferred (again free of charge) to the Commonwealth. The second step (with which Schumacher was very much involved) was to help to develop the constitution with his new partners – the former employees – to clarify the responsibility for the 'bundle of powers' previously held by private ownership. The constitution defined the "self-denying ordinances", deliberately restricting certain aspects of the company's development. These are worth enumerating since, almost 50 years later, they are still flying in the face of contemporary developments and yet could be of significant value to other companies wishing to take the same democratic route.

First – the size of the company should not grow beyond 350-400 persons so that each one can relate in his or her mind to the organisation as a whole. If later circumstances demanded further expansion, a separate fully independent company would be set up alongside the Scott Bader Commonwealth. (It was not long before there were three such companies.)

Second – Ideally, remuneration for work within the organisation should not vary greatly beyond a certain level whatever anyone's age, sex, experience and function. This nevertheless still worked out at a range of 1:7 before tax and quickly became 1:12. [There is now no clear policy on pay differentials.]

Third – As Members of the Commonwealth were all co-owners and partners, no one could be dismissed other than for gross personal misconduct. Naturally, anyone was free to leave by giving proper notice.

Fourth – A sort of 'parliament of workers' or Council was the sovereign body, and the Company's Board of Directors was fully accountable to them. The Commonwealth members could confirm or withdraw their appointment and agree their remuneration. This Council was responsible to the Commonwealth Members.

Fifth – Up to 40% of net profits would be apportioned to the Commonwealth, with a minimum 60% being retained for taxation and for self-finance, research and development of the operating Company. Any bonuses for the Members must be matched by funding for charitable purposes in the local community and abroad. In addition to the enrichment of local facilities, such as sports grounds, the profits enabled workers to set up communal workshops to repair their own cars and machinery, with such additions as garden and mechanical maintenance 'tool pools' to facilitate their leisure activities and hobbies.

Sixth – None of the products of the company should be sold to customers with known war-related purposes.

When these revolutionary ideas were introduced, the financial world was astonished, as it judged that a private company based on co-ownership and self-imposed ethics and democracy could not survive. In fact, despite certain difficulties, crises and setbacks, and despite the highly competitive market in its operating field, this small company went from strength to strength, increasing its sales almost tenfold. As Fritz later remarked, what was intended as an experiment in the humanisation of work (which was only partly achieved) actually became a way of life. The challenging idea was to transfer ownership from one person to a 'family of co-workers' and to develop ideas on the role of trusteeship. This, in effect, changed the existential character of ownership and involved them all grappling together with the new and constantly evolving structures. It also accentuated the idea of connectedness, interdependence and awareness of the various needs of individuals, the company and the wider community environment.

The Scott Bader Commonwealth still flourishes today, ever developing to meet the needs of new clients, technologies and materials. Schumacher's presence on the Board gave this innovative company a stimulus, and at the same time enabled him to develop his own ideas on ownership. In the words of Godric Bader, Ernest's son and successor:

> *"Fritz's originality and his DNA are embodied in the company as we attempt to put true democracy at the heart of all our operations. . . . I would like to think that the 21st-century description we are beginning to use to describe Scott Bader, as a 'Democratic Trusteeship', owes much to Schumacher's innovative ideas. One such idea (which was unfortunately rejected) was hiring a team of biologists to experiment with ways to develop plastics from plant materials as petroleum-based substitutes. In this we missed a valuable opportunity, as has subsequently been shown. The Commonwealth's responsibility for a 'bundle of assets' instead of ownership of them, has a direct parallel as to how we now urgently have to look at our earthly home . . . the 'bundle of assets' being the air, sea and land through which Nature and our life have evolved and are sustained."* [4]

The proliferation of small-scale organisations within large-scale industry

Throughout Fritz Schumacher's work, lectures and writings runs the consistent emphasis on quality rather than quantity; on community; and on local empowerment whenever self-organisation at the local level was feasible. This would seem to make his models useful guidelines for David Cameron's ideas on devolution and 'The Big Society', as well as for any other political systems reaching towards localism.

Although emphasising the potential creativity and flexibility of small organisations and units, he did concede that there were certain essential national services which needed to be nationalised and should be run for the benefit of all users rather than for the shareholders. These included the power industries, water supply and transport industries, and the national health and social services. As an ardent young socialist, whose thinking had contributed to much post-war reconstruction, he naturally favoured public rather than private ownership, believing that even national utility supply industries could also be run on a regional basis.

After 1973, with the added incentive of a fourfold rise in the price of oil, Schumacher's economic common sense was at last seen as having some relevance to a few larger, established industries in Europe and the US. However, this interest only lasted as long as the oil crisis, and his ideas are now being rekindled once again, partly because of 'peak oil' and fears of future energy shortfalls. Below are two early examples of attempts to put 'appropriate scale' thinking into practice in big industry, neither of which was sustained at the time.

Lucas Aerospace

A typical example of how some of Schumacher's ideas gradually percolated through to UK industry, but failed to take root, was the experience of a small group of engineers working for Lucas Aerospace in Bradford and Leeds in the early 1970s. At that time the company was seeking to diversify out of the defence industry, where markets were extremely volatile and subject to international politics and changing policies of governments. Spearheading this approach was a small interdisciplinary team under the enthusiastic leadership of Terry Simms, an experienced electrical engineer who had a broad brief to explore various potential opportunities. His approach was all-inclusive, and in part was based upon the seminal ideas contained in *Small is Beautiful* which he had just read. The challenge was to adapt Lucas engineers' skills and specialist knowledge to solving problems encountered by other industries which were further down the technical scale but came under the Lucas umbrella. Some industries examined included textiles, forging, sugar production, machine tools and even nuclear fuel enrichment. The engineers' group did succeed in developing new products and solutions in several of these fields, but unfortunately the parent company showed no interest in encouraging the ideas further or supplying the necessary investments. The diversification attempt was eventually abandoned.

In parallel with the engineers' work, Mike Cooley, a leading shop steward at Lucas, started the Shop Stewards Alternative Corporate Plan. Influenced by Schumacher's 'lifeboat' thinking, Cooley's was a proactive attempt to avoid the closure of Lucas factories by identifying socially useful products for the company to manufacture. In the event, Lucas management was not ready to undertake such a radical foray into new markets and so rejected the Alternative Corporate Plan. The only products created through its own diversification efforts were merely used to add value to other parts of the company before disposal. Thus, after some limited further developments and initial marketing, both the Lucas initiatives were shelved as the company cut down on its R&D budget. These attempts to provide 'lifeboats' for vulnerable large industries were unfortunately ahead of their time.

AT-ITDG

At the same time another, albeit unrelated, initiative was taken by Dr John Davis of Shell International, who had met up with Schumacher after the publication of *Small is Beautiful*. He had also been greatly inspired by the Horizon film *The Other Way*, which had portrayed Schumacher's work using UK examples from industry by way of illustration. All this publicity about Schumacher's vision for industry prompted Davis to form a core support group for a programme of work based on putting some of Schumacher's ideas into practice in Shell UK. This initiative was linked to the Intermediate Technology Development Group (ITDG) as it was then called (see Chapter 3). The UK-based project was named Appropriate Technology or AT. The group addressed itself to 'economic development as though people mattered' in the UK by tackling the twin problems of factory closures and the need for a community-based approach to energy conservation and waste recycling.

Local Enterprise Trusts

The first of these initiatives led to the creation of Local Enterprise Trusts, which grew to 36 in number in areas of high unemployment, creating over 50,000 jobs by 1981. There were almost 200 Local Enterprise Trusts in operation throughout the UK by 1985. Brian Padgett, who had been a member of the original multi-disciplinary industrial team at Lucas and had joined John Davis's Appropriate Technology Group in 1980 comments:

> *"The programme of appropriate technology in the UK which John Davis founded . . . consisted of helping the formation of local initiatives throughout the UK, each the creation of its own local community and independent of the Central Group. Evidence of their success and best practice was cross-fertilised between the trusts by means of a newsletter circulated also to MPs and other opinion formers.*
>
> *Thus the problem created by the factory closures, common in the 1960s and 1970s and first addressed by Mike Cooley in his pre-closure Alternative Corporate Plan, was now being tackled post-closures by the Local Enterprise Trusts."* [5]

These Trusts eventually led to the formation of Business in the Community,[6] which is still a flourishing concern today with a membership of 850 companies ranging from large multinationals to small local businesses and public sector organisations. Members are advised and encouraged to create a sustainable future for humans and the environment through responsible business practice and to share their information and experiences through this powerful network, of which the Prince of Wales is President.

Local Energy Groups

Local Energy Groups were formed by those concerned about the waste of energy and raw materials at a local level, as a parallel development to the Local Enterprise Trusts. Unfortunately these groups also were ahead of their time. With higher employment levels and the resumption of cheaper fuels after the oil crises of the 1970s, the grassroots energy initiatives flagged. It is only now, in the 21st century, with the imminent threat of climate change and again with rising fuel prices, that the urgent message of energy conservation and local recycling is once more finding widespread support with government, industry, communities and the public alike.

Technology Exchange Ltd

In 1985, with the help of John Davis, George McRobie, Mike Cooley, Gordon Morrell from ICI and others, Brian Padgett founded the Technology Exchange Ltd as a company limited by guarantee. This initiative also stemmed from the UK Programme of ITDG and was directly linked to Schumacher's thinking about matching up innovation with the specific needs of industry elsewhere. From 1990 to 1992 details of over 10,000 new developments from 35 countries were brought to the attention of manufacturers in the UK, and firms from 53 countries took part in these technology exchange initiatives. Later, with the United Nations Industrial Development Organisation (UNIDO), the scope of the work was extended to create partnerships for firms in Africa, China, Vietnam, India and Brazil with firms in the developed world.

Schumacher had always believed that any new and beneficial improvements in technology should be made widely available to all who needed them. Technology Exchange therefore decided that this could best be done by non-exclusive licensing rights, to enable the cost of development to be recovered, and further improvements to be funded. These were the primary objectives that the Technology Exchange organisation, in the spirit of Schumacher, sought to achieve. It was hoped that in future the organisation would provide a model for international technology co-operation between firms in tackling the twin problems of energy scarcity and preservation of the environment on a global scale.

This sharing of technology between industries and nations allows cleaner and more energy-efficient technologies to be more widely utilised and, where applied, to minimise the impact of a growing world population on the environment. From the present time onwards it would seem that cost alone cannot be the main deciding factor, as it has been in the past. In future, the technology choice to be made in each case will surely be one where only the most energy-efficient and least environmentally harmful will be acceptable.

These have been a few examples of how Schumacher's vision for industry has been translated into action, originally through a network of people with whom he had some direct or indirect personal contact. However, despite recognition of the benefits of these innovative approaches, it must be acknowledged that in terms of practical achievements, his ideas have so far made much more of an impact in Third World countries than in the industrialised ones. Instead of companies diversifying their interests to decrease their vulnerability in times of crisis, they are increasingly taken over by ever larger transnational corporations with no particular concern for the well-being of either their workforce or the communities in which they operate. It is only with current industrial and socio-economic systems crumbling and threatening the complacent lifestyles of the industrialised world, that an integrated and inclusive interest in sustainable local employment initiatives, and in long-term local resource and energy-saving management, is again being rekindled.

Chapter 8

The relevance of
E. F. Schumacher today

"Truth has not special time of its own. Its hour is now – always, and indeed then most truly, when it seems most unsuitable to actual circumstances." – Albert Schweitzer

In highlighting certain aspects of Fritz Schumacher's thinking and the various initiatives outlined in the preceding pages, what conclusions can we draw? How are his ideas still relevant as we face the interrelated global crises of the 21st century? Each of the organisations described in this Briefing has had a very significant influence in its prescribed field of activity. And each in some way is directly linked to the ideas of Schumacher and bears the hallmark of his holistic thinking. Moreover, each of these initiatives, in turn, has created ripples and waves which, have spread far afield, influencing thought and action in a great many areas not always directly connected with Schumacher himself.

These developments range from Wangari Maathai's Green Belt Movement in Africa,[1] to Vandana Shiva's Navdanya International in India,[2] to the worldwide Transition movement already described. There is a growing Buddhist Economics movement in the Far East, propagated by the Thai Buddhist Sulak Sivaraksa, and in Europe this is spearheaded by the University of Budapest. There is also some interest in Buddhist economics in certain parts of the USA. However, all these important movements originally sprang from small initiatives. This demonstrates, yet again, how even small committed groups of people can help to effect widespread change.

While each organisation represented under the 'Schumacher umbrella' can make a significant impact in its own field, in the future all will need to work much more closely together and to connect with a much wider public and with decision-makers at every level to ensure that there can be sustainable and lasting change. This applies to organisations in both industrial and developing countries. Industry, despite all its material and technological assets, has become too complex and fragmented. The developing world, on the other hand, too frequently lacks adequate facilities for education, for improving technical skills, and for providing sufficient material means and the necessary basic infrastructure. These endemic problems of the First and Third Worlds can still be addressed very positively, with diligent application of the knowledge and resources available today. What is required now is an imaginative and intuitive re-envisioning of how a healthy society might function, and a reordering of priorities.

Schumacher understood that the various aspects of human activity had become too divorced from spiritual values and their associated disciplines to be able to effect the behavioural changes that are needed. We must now abandon the long-cherished idols of acquisitiveness, unrestrained growth, power, economic globalisation and so forth, and replace them with the more permanent ideals of humility, frugality and responsibility for the wellbeing of future generations and of the environment. The necessary changes in human behaviour still include drastically reducing our expectations as consumers of the Earth's resources, and a willingness to place the needs of the poor and powerless alongside our own.

Even to begin this transformative process requires courage, optimism, vision, co-operation and the ability of each individual, organisation or institution to actively adopt the concept of sufficiency or 'enough'. With today's scientific and technical knowledge, and with continued development especially in the fields of renewable energy, energy efficiency and food production, the Earth's resources could readily provide "enough for everyone's need but not for everyone's greed".

Where the habit of 'enough' prevails, a culture of peace can begin to take root as a way of life, thus reducing the threat of violence and the need for wasteful and unecological investments in security and defence devices. Currently, some of the main growth industries in the UK are in 'negative' products such as armaments, crime prevention and detection mechanisms including burglar alarms and CCTV cameras, as well as in drugs, insurance and unreal financial 'products'. In a stable and socially trusting society, these industries can gradually be replaced by more positive, rewarding and productive ventures and socially enhancing goods and services. They might include better social and health care; amenity parks; local food production schemes; cultural and artistic productions and activities; community allotments; neighbourhood enterprises and other intergenerational activities which will involve the young and old alike. In fact, money would be released from investments in the 'negative' industries and activities necessitated by a dysfunctional society and could be channelled into creating worthwhile work, and providing the means to help to build up vibrant and caring local communities.

This vision, articulated by Schumacher in his own way, may at present seem utopian. However, as we stare into the abyss of the biggest man-made catastrophe the planet has ever known, such fundamental changes are surely preferable to the alternative. The human species can surely consciously change the course it has unwittingly set in motion – although this will not be done by applying the same economic orthodoxy as in the past. Unfortunately, faith in the future is still mainly vested in large and unaffordable schemes based on science and technology. These include unrealistic geo-engineering projects, carbon capture and storage (CCS) systems, and even advanced space exploration with a view to future colonisation of some planet which may be capable of supporting human life once the Earth is no longer able to do so. These are all rather more violent and capital-intensive aspects of the old 'business as usual' philosophy. Sadly, the whole apparatus of institutional thinking still appears to be wedded to large-scale, highly technical and nationally unaffordable solutions to problems of a completely different order. Most of our current crises have arisen through wrong thinking, leading to wrong decisions, since economics, rather than environmental concerns, always takes precedence in government policies. As has been demonstrated, our entire economic system is still based on an outmoded model of perpetual growth which is unsustainable and out of harmony with the natural order. This can only be reversed by a changed consciousness and changed priorities.

Part of Schumacher's legacy has been to recognise that unless we alter our lifestyles, we shall only expedite our own demise, along with destroying much of a very beautiful, self-regulating natural creation. In the cosmic order, humans can never become Masters of the Universe. Their unique attributes can, nevertheless, be applied in countless creative, scientific and intelligent ways to co-operate with nature and to use their very considerable gifts sustainably. Perhaps, as he suggested mischievously, a positive first step would be again to re-educate the young in the Christian cardinal virtues of justice, temperance, prudence and fortitude. We might now also add: to apply the disciplines of moderation, frugality and voluntary simplicity in the place of instant gratification of material wants or overstimulation by constant activity.

Schumacher's spiritual vision also included educating for a culture of non-violence, which implies instilling co-operation as opposed to competition. Again, many of his ideas on the subject were modelled on those of Mahatma Gandhi. There has to be an early recognition that no single person, however talented, gifted or educated, can be complete by himself or herself. Life has been ordered in such a way that everyone is interdependent and is designed to live and work harmoniously and in community. Schumacher himself practised non-violence as an educative way of life, including a non-violent attitude to politics, to economics, to agriculture, towards the environment and towards his fellow humans. Such perspectives need to be grounded at a very early age, and hence the paramount importance of a balanced education.

In educating young people, Schumacher stressed that there has to be a differentiation between the accumulation of facts and knowledge, the development of better intuitive understanding, and the cultivation of wisdom. In the words of the old Chinese proverb 'Education is to grow a garden, not to fill a barrel.' The emphasis needs to shift from absorbing and quantifying data to assessing its quality and intrinsic value, as well evaluating how it can best be applied. While these aspects all are necessary for the development of the whole person, the current focus in education is largely on the former, with a view to passing examinations rather than to producing balanced, well-adjusted citizens. The statistics on child delinquency, drug abuse and depression demonstrate, only too clearly, this imbalance. It is possible that with less stress and pressure on achieving goals, young people would be happier and more relaxed contributors to social well-being. There needs to be a re-ordering of educational values, and a challenging of basic assumptions, to ensure that the ends always justify the means.

Schumacher frequently drew attention to the numerous problems stemming from wrong priorities. Challenging situations are frequently addressed by superficial and expensive solutions which take no account of their real causes. Today we have plentiful examples. In the current financial meltdown, we are being encouraged to spend our way out of the financial crisis in a world of diminishing resources and in the face of global warming. At the same time we are exhorted to conserve energy and reduce our personal carbon footprint. The conflicting official policies of world leaders hardly ever confront the underlying issues or take the appropriate long-term measures. As Lester Brown, Founder and President of the Washington-based WorldWatch Institute, has critically remarked on several occasions, in the face of global warming, governments need to put their economies and those of their citizens onto a wartime footing. This involves only allowing the production, marketing and distribution of those commodities and services which are absolutely necessary and beneficial for national sustainability and the health and wellbeing of society. If environmentally damaging goals and activities are closed down, jobs can be diverted into sustainable production and services such as the insulation of buildings, installing renewable energy devices and expanding and maintaining local amenities. Studies have demonstrated that each pound invested in such activities creates considerably more local employment than an equivalent investment in the large-scale, centrally controlled power industries, many of which put people out of work which, in turn, puts a burden on families and the social services.

The whole question of fuel, food and finance and their interrelationship looms large in the present day, as it did in Schumacher's time. It is to the UK's great cost that hitherto little concerted action has been taken by any government to develop a coherent integrated national strategy in this respect. However, there are at last signs that with the Climate Change Act of October 2008, legally binding the UK to cut CO_2 emissions by 80% by 2050, and the Coalition Government's emphasis on 'The Big Society', there may emerge genuine new policies for local economic self-reliance in the fields of energy and food production. Hopefully these will not merely be driven by short-term political expediency, but will also create more reliable long-term local employment and economic activity at grassroots level.

As we stand at this crossroads in history, it is essential that politicians and those in power vigorously adopt some of Schumacher's long-term sustainability principles when they make political and economic decisions which will affect the future of all. These include his recommendations on maintaining biodiversity in all the key areas of farming, food production, agroforestry and fuel. His ideas on work organisation and the development of local co-operatives are also extremely socially just and beneficial, and would help to maintain local resilience in times of crisis.

In the field of energy, many innovative and other new developments have taken place in recent years. Today, most industrial countries are investing heavily in renewable energy schemes. The European Union currently employs over half a million people in this sector. These industries deliver more jobs per unit of investment than an equivalent investment in fossil-fuel technologies. Apart from the initial production plant and transmission systems, they are also carbon-neutral and the systems can be locally maintained.

Renewable innovations under construction include solar panel aqua farms which are being installed on lakes and reservoirs, thus supplying local electricity without taking up valuable land space.[3] These consist of arrays of photovoltaic cells situated on floating pontoons with underwater transmission lines and are providing great investment opportunities across the globe, from Australia, California, China and India to the Middle East. Even EDF (Electricité de France), the world's largest utility company, is installing solar aqua farms on some of its nuclear cooling ponds.

New energy conservation prototypes are also under development. 'Smart cities' are being built, which rely on solar power, energy-efficient buildings, revolutionary transport systems and the reuse of all waste materials. An example is Madsen City near Abu Dhabi, an experimental offshoot of the Massachusetts Institute of Technology. There is also a growing number of designated 'solar cities' worldwide, especially in India, China and Australia, and a surprisingly large number of pioneering examples in Europe. An example is Seville's PSO Solar Tower: when the project is completed it will generate over 300MW of electricity from renewable sources, thus creating 1,000 jobs and saving 600,000 tonnes of CO_2 p.a.[4] In many regions worldwide, renewable biomass oil substitutes such as ethanol are also being developed on a large scale, although these are not entirely carbon-neutral and are creating a certain amount of environmental controversy. As early as the 1960s Schumacher was investigating the potential of biomass as a substitute for fossil fuels. Evidently, he did not foresee the future 'fuel or food' debate, where there is pressure on the land.

For some years the UK has been pioneering offshore wind farms, as well as the arrays of wind turbines more commonly situated on hillsides and mountains. In 2009 Scottish Power Renewables completed Europe's largest land-based wind farm at Whitelee near Glasgow. With a planned capacity of 614MW, this will power the homes of Glasgow's 600,000 inhabitants and supply 40% of the City's total electricity consumption. There are plans to develop a vast offshore wind farm off the west coast of Scotland, at least five or six times the size of the Whitelee wind farm. Meanwhile the London Array is being constructed in the Thames Estuary about 12 miles off the coasts of Kent and Essex. With a planned 1,000MW capacity, this is expected to be the world's largest offshore wind farm, with the first 175 turbines due for completion before the London Olympics in 2012. When finished, the London Array will displace 1.9 million tonnes of CO_2 emissions and is a vital part of the UK's plan to cut these by 80% by 2050. Other major offshore wind projects are planned off the Suffolk coast once the environmental impact assessments have been carried out.[5]

Schumacher was an enthusiastic advocate of promising new renewable energy technologies. However, fossil fuels undoubtedly will be required to carry us through the transition period, but, given the limited availability in a world of growing demands and the ever-increasing cost of accessing them, theirs will be a restricted and economically unfavourable future. After the recent Fukushima disaster in Japan, and in the wake of the ongoing pollution from the 1986 Chernobyl accident and other less publicised nuclear incidents, it is not difficult to see why Fritz was so fiercely opposed to the potential violence of the nuclear energy option. The fact that the power source is centralised, unaffordable to the Third World poor and that there is, as yet, no safe way to contain and store the extremely long-term radioactive wastes, still makes this an unsafe energy investment option. Nevertheless, the nuclear power plants currently in operation may still be supplying electricity until the transition to alternative sources of energy takes place. As Germany has demonstrated, the policy of replacing nuclear energy with alternative sources is a matter of government decision. What is now urgently needed is for energy supplies to be more democratic, and for serious investment in technology transfer to new, more sophisticated renewable energy systems in order to bring down production costs so that these systems become more readily available for all. The skills of engineers and maintenance workers in this field need to be upgraded. There has been astonishingly little investment in this area compared with the fossil-fuel industries, and more especially nuclear power. There is need also for a global technology investment fund from the north to the south to supply local communities with new, more efficient and environmentally clean energy.

The central issue of food, and the feeding of an ever-increasing world population, remain the unsolved global problems that they were when addressed by Fritz Schumacher. Undoubtedly his advocacy of organic farming, forest gardens and biodynamic agriculture is an extremely positive contribution. However, unless there is more equitable distribution of wealth, land and resources worldwide, the poor will continue to be deprived of their rightful livelihood. We must also acknowledge the fundamental need for education, know-how and access to basic technologies, of which Schumacher was only too well aware.

There is a great danger of freezing an iconic figure such as Schumacher in the situation of their time, and not allowing for the fact that his ideas would have been constantly evolving in changing circumstances. Some of his predictions, such as the date at which world oil supplies might peak, have proved incorrect owing to the discovery of vast oil and gas reserves under the oceans. Other relevant issues, such as the population explosion, he simply failed to address at the time. He believed that the latter would solve itself if people could only be lifted out of poverty and become better educated. At the same time he always endeavoured to seek out new information and new solutions to new phenomena as they arose, whilst personally practising the art of 'living in the present moment'. The revolutions in information technology, nanotechnology, virtual reality, genetic engineering and geo-engineering – issues which have arisen during the last 35 years – would have undoubtedly occupied Schumacher's attention insofar as they affect our overall human condition. Nevertheless, he repeatedly warned against the unseen perils of pollution, of the inherent dangers of nuclear power and the probability of a major nuclear accident occurring – although up to the time of his death, all reported nuclear incidents had been comparatively minor ones.

Some people may judge that Fritz Schumacher's philosophy and his practical thinking, with its focus on local sustainability in terms of work, food and fuel, are now archaic. The current emphasis is on the continued march towards economic centralisation, facilitated by a revolution in new realms of technology which he never lived to see. Nevertheless, his proposed systems-level solutions reflected his direct life experience in the industrial world, and his attempts to set up support systems for Third World communities living in poverty and degradation. His attitude, albeit sometimes impatient, was in essence one of simplicity towards the management of our natural resources, and humility in our demands on the environment. It was a long-term perspective which took account of the interrelationships, both known and unknown, which exist at every level. His faith was in the intrinsic goodness of people, and all his thinking was based on a deep personal spirituality founded on traditional wisdom and his own Christian religious faith. His was a wake-up call to a new generation in whose hands the future of humanity now rests. Today this is an even more urgent call to awaken an intensified consciousness, and an awareness which is all-inclusive and well beyond all bounds of class, colour or creed.

As I write this in the year in which we celebrate the centenary of Schumacher's birth, it is curious to note that many of his most fundamental concepts regarding human-scale organisations have never yet been applied at a systematic practical level in the West. As we have seen, these included regionally based systems for food production, energy generation and economic activity in general; recognition of the true value of work; ensuring the proper end-use of all natural resources; safeguarding biodiversity at all levels; and a long-term custodianship of the land. There has been some progress in certain areas, but this is by no means universal or co-ordinated. One of Schumacher's personal observations was that people generally change either through insight or through suffering: we now may not have much choice! With the current interrelated ecological, economic and societal crises which challenge the very roots of industrial society as well as the developing world, it is evident that we now have a great opportunity for change through necessity. The transition, over 30 years on is not at all an easy one but may well be forced upon us by external conditions.

As food and fuel scarcity threaten even the rich nations, and as natural disasters, frequently caused by global warming, affect rich and poor alike, we would be well advised to prepare for possible social and economic collapse by re-examining some of Schumacher's community-based solutions and survival strategies. Previous chapters will hopefully have provided some useful guidelines as to how regional communities and organisations can adapt. Although we have lost far too many years, the technologies and opportunities already exist, as in the case of renewable energy. What is needed is more government investment in the technical skills and delivery systems to implement these. They might also help in the creation of a more wholesome and sustainable 'economics of permanence'.

It is with such issues that the various Schumacher Circle members have sought to occupy themselves over the past few decades, but the time has now come for a much broader social and environmental movement embracing as many people as possible. After delays in reaching realistic international agreement on environmental action in Copenhagen and Cancun, people everywhere are refocusing on taking action through the workplace, local communities and civil society groups. This applies especially to energy issues, which underpin all Western lifestyles. In the words of Paul Allen, Director of the Centre for Alternative Technology, "This energy transition is the cornerstone of a new economic approach which will move Britain on from doing the things which got us into trouble in the first place."

There is currently a whole galaxy of new ideas and actions which are now changing attitudes at local community level, as exemplified by the Transition movement. These include local self-reliance initiatives; community food and energy production systems; land-, labour- and equipment-sharing schemes, and encouraging people to change their attitudes towards local innovation and to take personal responsibility for reducing their consumption of material resources. All are aspects of Schumacher's philosophy of voluntary simplicity to enhance and enrich wellbeing at an individual as well as community level. Unless the necessary changes are put in motion immediately, the outcome of our irrational and irreverential behaviour towards energy and nature's other life support systems will sadly be inherited by the next generation. For them it will be too late.

As we take stock of our current situation, we see that most of the problems which Schumacher addressed are unfortunately still with us, and many of these have since been greatly exacerbated. We urgently need to revisit some of those prophetic 'maps' and guidelines which he left behind. His 'solutions' are based on the principle of 'interconnectedness' and on deep spiritual values which have stood the test of time and have sustained people, planet and the natural order over the centuries. Although the clouds on the horizon may seem dark, it is now time to start afresh by trying out new imaginative ways of working, beginning with ourselves, our families, and those people whom we love and know. As Schumacher observed in *Good Work*:

> "*I certainly never feel discouraged. I can't myself raise the winds which might blow us, or this ship into a better world. But I can at least put up the sail, so that when the wind comes I can catch it.*"

Perhaps that wind is on its way here now – and we must be ready!

Notes*

Chapter 1: Who was E. F. Schumacher?

1. See Barbara Wood's biography of her father, *Alias Papa: a life of Fritz Schumacher*. Jonathan Cape, London 1984 (new edition by Green Books, 2011).
2. Kohr, Leopold and Schumacher, E. F. *A Pair of Cranks*, edited by John Papworth. New European Publications.
3. Schuon, Fritjof. *The Transcendent Unity of Religions*. Quest Books, USA.
4. For several years Fritz attended meditation classes based on the ideas of Gurdjieff and Ouspensky.
5. 'Buddhist Economics' first appeared in an article for *Resurgence* magazine in 1968. It is frequently referred to in this Briefing, having influenced many organisations worldwide.
6. *On the Edge of the Forest* is available as a DVD from nicola@efschumacher.co.uk.
7. Schumacher, E. F. (1973). *Small is Beautiful: A Study of Economics as if People Mattered*. Abacus.
8. McRobie, George (1981). *Small is Possible*. Jonathan Cape.
9. Schumacher, E. F. (1977). *A Guide for the Perplexed*. Jonathan Cape.
10. Schumacher, E. F. (1979). *Good Work*. Jonathan Cape.
11. Kirk, Geoffrey (1982). *Schumacher on Energy*. Jonathan Cape.
12. Schumacher, E. F. (1997). *This I Believe and Other Essays*. Green Books.

Chapter 2: The Schumacher Society

1. Schumacher, E. F. (1973). *Small is Beautiful*. Abacus. Chapter 6.
2. Illich, Ivan (1971). *Deschooling Society*. Calder & Boyars.
3. Schumacher, E. F. (1973). *Small is Beautiful*. Abacus.
4. Kumar, Satish (ed.) (1980). *The Schumacher Lectures Vol.I*. Blond & Briggs.
5. Kumar, Satish (ed.) (1984). *The Schumacher Lectures Vol.II*. Blond & Briggs.
6. Hopkins, Rob (2008). *The Transition Handbook: from oil dependency to local resilience*. Green Books.
7. The Small School. www.smallschoolathartland.org.
8. Capra, Fritjof (2008), in Phillips, Anne. *Holistic Education: learning from Schumacher College*. Green Books. See also www.schumachercollege.org.

---

* Available in PDF format with live links on the Green Books website at http://www.greenbooks.co.uk/Book/396/Small-is-Beautiful-in-the-21st-Century.html

9. Pontin, John & Roderick, Ian (2007). *Converging World: Connecting Communities in Global Change*. Schumacher Briefing No. 13. Green Books.
10. Pontin, John & Roderick, Ian (2008), in John Blewitt (ed.) *Community, Empowerment and Sustainable Development*. Green Books.

Chapter 3: Third World development models

1. Schumacher's address to the World Moral Rearmament Conference in Caux, Switzerland on the day of his death, September 4th 1977.
2. Ibid.
3. See http://practicalaction.org/climatechange_adaptation.
4. Jeevika Trust, www.jeevika.org.uk.
5. ATDA is now Schumacher Centre for Development. See www.schumacherindia.org.

Chapter 4: Food, agriculture and land use

1. Drawn up by Dr S. L. Mansholt, President of the European Economic Community. The plan was the forerunner of the ill-fated Common Agricultural Policy (CAP).
2. Schumacher, E. F. (1973). *Small is Beautiful*. Abacus. pp.90-93.
3. Henry Doubleday Research Association (now called Garden Organic): www.gardenorganic.org.uk. See also Quality Low Input Food Project: www.ncl.ac.uk/tcoa/qlif.html.
4. E. F. Schumacher, Soil Association 25th Anniversary Conference, 1971.
5. The Soil Association, www.soilassociation.org.
6. Hopkins, Rob (2008). *The Transition Handbook*. Green Books.
7. St Barbe Baker, Richard (1986). *My Life, My Trees*. Findhorn Press.
8. Tree Aid, www.treeaid.org.uk.
9. Rose, Sir Julian (private correspondence). International Coalition to Protect the Polish Countryside (ICPPC), Mi dzynarodowa Koalicja dla Ochrony Polskiej Wsi 34-146 Stryszów 156, Poland. Tel./fax +48 33 8797114. biuro@icppc.pl www.icppc.pl, www.gmo.icppc.pl, www.eko-cel.pl.
10. Centre for Ecoliteracy, www.ecoliteracy.org.
11. Navdanya Project, www.navdanya.org.
12. Shiva, Vandana (2008). *Soil Not Oil: Climate Change, Peak Oil and Food Insecurity*. Zed Books. p.3.
13. Report of the International Assessment of Agricultural Science and Technology for Development (IAASTD). www.agassessment-watch.org

Chapter 5: Small-scale technologies for local sustainability

1. Gerard Morgan-Grenville sadly died in March 2009, but had always remained in close contact with CAT since its beginning and also with the Schumacher Society. He was a true Renaissance character – author, painter, music lover, raconteur, social and business entrepreneur (he managed to successfully combine both) and 'bon viveur'! As one of the founder members of the Green Alliance, and the Ecological Action Group for Europe as well as the Schumacher Society and countless other organisations, his presence will be surely missed by all pioneers in the European environmental movement.
2. For further information see www.cat.org.uk.
3. Aber Instruments, www.aber-instruments.co.uk.
4. Dulas Engineering, www.dulasltd.co.uk,
5. Ecodyfi, www.ecodyfi.org.uk.
6. Rocky Mountain Institute, www.rmi.org.
7. The Findhorn Foundation, www.findhorn.org.
8. The Eden Project, www.edenproject.com.

Chapter 6: The call for a new economics

1. Schumacher, E. F. (1973). *Small is Beautiful*. Abacus.
2. Ekins, Paul (1986). *The Living Economy: A New Economics in the Making*. Routledge & Kegan Paul.
3. Simms, Andrew. 'From the Ashes of the Crash'. nef, www.neweconomics.org.
4. Spratt, Stephen and Wallis, Stewart. 'From Old Economics to New Economics: Radical Reform for a Sustainable Future'. nef, www.neweconomics.org.
5. Klein, Naomi (2007). *The Shock Doctrine*. Allen Lane / Penguin.
6. See www.happyplanetindex.org.
7. See www.nationalaccountsofwellbeing.org.
8. 'A Green New Deal' (2007). nef.
See www.neweconomics.org/projects/green-new-deal
9. Simms, A., Moran, D. and Chowla, P. (2006). 'The UK Interdependence Report: How the World Sustains the Nation's Lifestyles and the Price it Pays'. nef, www.neweconomics.org.
10. Ward, B. & Lewis, J. (2002). 'Plugging the Leaks', nef, www.pluggingtheleaks.org.
11. 'The Local Multiplier', nef, www.neweconomics.org.
12. Simms, Andrew et al., 'Clone Town Britain: The loss of local identity on the nation's high streets'. nef, www.neweconomics.org.

13. Schumacher, E. F. (1979). *Good Work*. Jonathan Cape.

14. Stephens, Lucie, Ryan-Collins, Josh & Boyle, David (2008). 'Co-production: a manifesto for growing the core economy'. Also Slay, Julia & Robinson, Ben (2011). 'In This Together, Building Knowledge about Co-Production'. nef, www.neweconomics.org.

15. Time Banks UK, www.timebanking.org.

16. See www.neweconomics.org/sites/neweconomics.org/files/Good_Banking.pdf.

17. 'The Ratio: common sense controls for executive pay and revitalising UK business' (2011). nef, www.neweconomics.org.

18. 'The Ethical Purchasing Index' (EPI). nef, www.neweconomics.org.

19. The E.F. Schumacher Society (USA), www.smallisbeautiful.org.

20. The New Economics Institute, http://neweconomicsinstitute.org.

21. Michael Gordon is the Outreach Co-ordinator for the New Economics Institute (USA). www.smallisbeautiful.org.

22. Fullerton, John (2008). 'The relevance of Schumacher in the 21st Century'. Article submitted for this Briefing, subsequently published by the E. F. Schumacher Society.

Chapter 7: Transforming industrial work in the First World

1. Schumacher, E. F. (1973). *Small is Beautiful* (Epilogue). Abacus.

2. Schumacher, E. F. (1979). *Good Work*. Jonathan Cape. Prologue. Also Hoe, Susanna (1978). *The Man Who Gave His Company Away*. Heinemann.

3. Bader, Godric, quoted from an article about his father for this Briefing, 2008.

4. Private correspondence with the author, 2008.

5. Padgett, Brian, private correspondence with the author, June 2008.

6. Business in the Community, www.bitc.org.uk.

Chapter 8: The relevance of E. F. Schumacher today

1. The Green Belt Movement, www.greenbeltmovement.org.

2. Navdanya, www.navdanya.org.

3. Todd, Woody. 'Solar Industry Sees a Future in Panels That Float on Water'. *New York Times*, Sunday, May 1, 2011.

4. Girardet, Herbert and Mendonça, Miguel (2009). *A Renewable World: Energy, Ecology, Equality. A report for the World Future Council*. Green Books.

5. Allen, Paul, in 'Supporters Update' (Spring 2011) of the Centre for Alternative Technology.

OTHER SCHUMACHER BRIEFINGS

For full details of all the Schumacher Briefings,
please see www.schumacher.org.uk or www.greenbooks.co.uk